Travel Guide

KYOTO

NARA
OSAKA
KOBE

*

英文京都案内

TRAVEL GUIDE
KYOTO
NARA OSAKA KOBE

First edition 1972
15th edition 1993

The photos in this book, except those taken by
the Japan Travel Bureau, Inc., are reproduced
through the courtesy of The Japan Travel Bureau Photo Library.

Printed in Japan
Photo Composition
by DEMPRO, Inc.
Printing
by Toppan Printing Co., Ltd.

KYOTO

Ninnaji Temple Five-Story Pagoda in Spring

Byōdōin

Nishi-Honganji Temple

Nembutsuji Temple

Kinkakuji Temple

Gion Matsuri

Jidai Matsuri

Kyoto Dancing

Aoi Matsuri

Kyōto Dishes

Traditional Bean Cakes

Bun-no-suke Jaya in Higashiyama

Maiko in Gion

Souvenir Stores in Sagano

Ishikawa Take-no-mise in Arashiyama

NARA

Hōryūji Temple Five-story Pagoda

Nara Park

Tōdaiji Temple, Daibutsuden

OSAKA

Dōtombori

KOBE

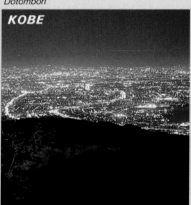

Night View

ISE

Woman Diver takes Pearl

Giōji Temple in Autumn

PREFACE

TRAVEL GUIDE: KYOTO, NARA, OSAKA, KOBE is intended to help the reader discover one of Japan's most important and well-known sightseeing areas -- the Kinki region. A useful travel companion, it is designed to make a visitor's stay here more enjoyable and more interesting.

The guide is divided into five main sections. The first three provide an introduction to the sights, shopping, dining and entertainment in the larger cities in the area while the last two sections give useful hints and practical information for the tourist. In addition, there is a handy reference index and lists of phone numbers and addresses.

We hope visitors will find this little book a useful and insightful guide that helps make their stay a very pleasant one.

JAPAN TRAVEL BUREAU, INC.

CONTENTS

KYOTO

OSAKA · KOBE

TRAVEL HINTS

NOTES

LETTERING

Japanese words, including personal names, are written in italics. Japanese personal names are written using the order used in English of given name, followed by family name. Pronunciation is indicated by a solid line over long vowels, e.g., shōgun.

DATA

Prices quoted are charges for adults and do not include tax or service charges. The required traveling times shown in the Area Guide are approximate times and are subject to seasonal changes, traffic and weather conditions, etc. Telephone numbers listed include the area code (the first 2 or more digits up to the first hyphen). Please omit the area code when making a local call. All data in this book is correct as of June, 1993.

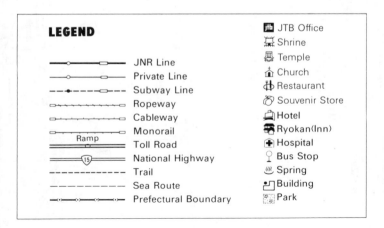

LEGEND

JNR Line	JTB Office
Private Line	Shrine
Subway Line	Temple
Ropeway	Church
Cableway	Restaurant
Monorail	Souvenir Store
Ramp / Toll Road	Hotel
National Highway (15)	Ryokan(Inn)
Trail	Hospital
Sea Route	Bus Stop
Prefectural Boundary	Spring
	Building
	Park

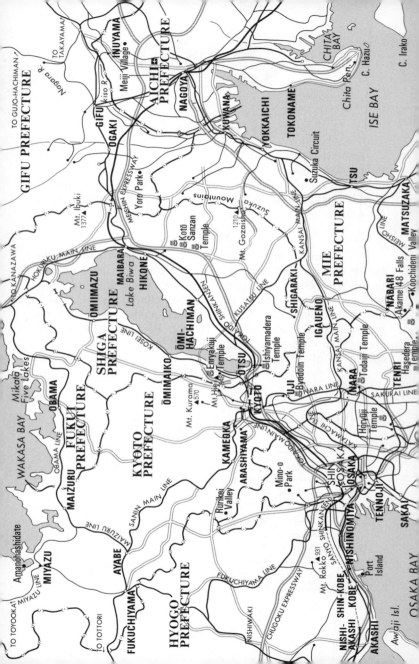

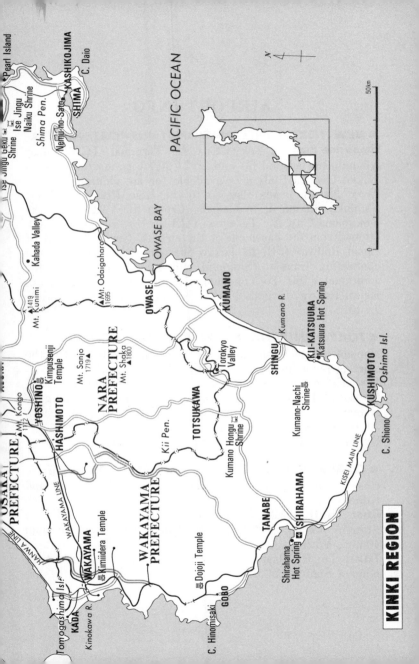

KINKI REGION

AIRPORT INFO

● **NEW TOKYO INTERNATIONAL AIRPORT: NARITA**
Limousine Bus: To Tokyo City Air Terminal (TCAT) near Nihombashi: around 60 min., ¥2,700. A connecting bus to Tokyo Central Station is available for an additional ¥100. From Narita, buses also go to the Keiō Plaza Hotel via Shinjuku Station or to Haneda Airport for ¥2,900. To the Yokohama City Air Terminal(YCAT): 1hr. 50min., ¥3,300.
Trains: From the basement of the airport, Narita Express of Japan Railway (JR) to Tokyo Station: 58min. ¥2,890 and connecting train to Shinjuku and Ikebukuro Station for additional ¥160. To Yokohama Station: 1hr. 35min. ¥4,100. Keisei Railway (private line) to Keisei Ueno Station: 1hr. ¥1,740.

● **TOKYO INTERNATIONAL AIRPORT: HANEDA**
Haneda is now used mainly by domestic airlines and is the starting point for air travel within Japan.
Taxi: From the downtown area ¥7,000 to ¥10,000.
Monorail: From the basement of the terminal building to Hamamatsu-chō Station in downtown Tokyo: 18 min., ¥300. At Hamamatsu-chō Station transfer to JR or taxi.
By air from Haneda to Osaka (1hr.): ¥14,600

● **OSAKA INTERNATIONAL AIRPORT**   The airport is close to the city and is the gateway to Osaka, Kyoto and Kobe.
Bus: To JR Osaka Station: 30min., ¥440. To JR Kyoto Station: 55min., ¥890. To JR Kobe Sannomiya Station: 40min., ¥720.
Taxi: To JR Osaka Station: ¥6,000. To JR Kobe Sannomiya Station: ¥9,000.

KYOTO

❖

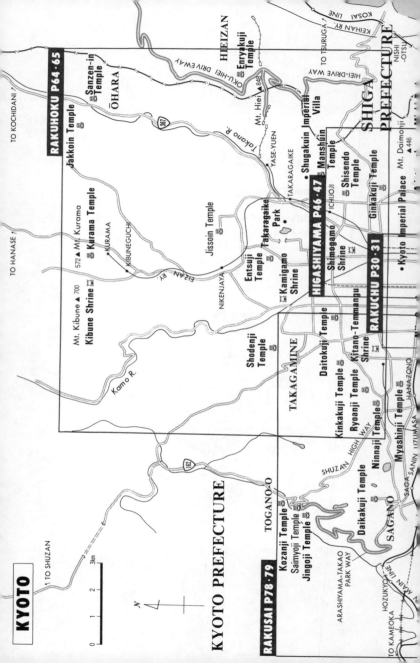

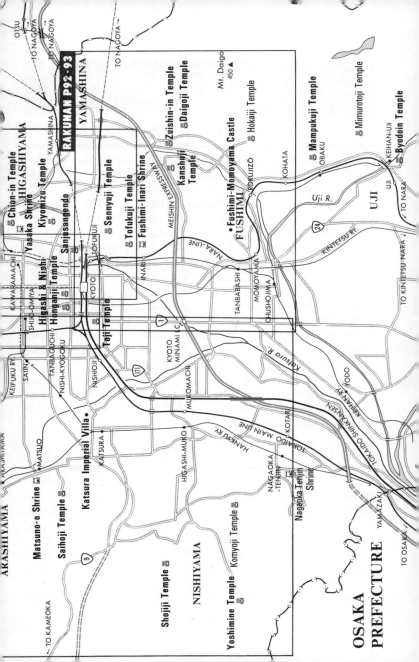

RAKUNAN P92·93

OSAKA PREFECTURE

AKASHIYAMA

ARASHIYAMA

Matsuno-o Shrine

Saihoji Temple

Katsura Imperial Villa

NISHIYAMA

Shojiji Temple

Yoshimine Temple

Komyoji Temple

Nagaoka-Tenjin Shrine

TO KAMEOKA

KEIFUKU RY.

SAIIN

MATSUO

KATSURA

NISHIOJI

TANBAGUCHI
NISHI-KYOGOKU

KAWARAMACHI

SHIJO-OMIYA

Higashi & Nishi Honganji Temple

Toji Temple

KYOTO

HIGASHIYAMA

Chion-in Temple

Yasaka Shrine

Kiyomizu Temple

Sanjusangendo

Sennyuji Temple

Tofukuji Temple

Fushimi-Inari Shrine

TOFUKUJI

INARI

NARA-LINE

MEISHIN EXPRESSWAY

YAMASHINA

OTSU

TO NAGOYA

TO NAGOYA

TO NAGOYA

YAMASHINA

Zuishin-in Temple

Daigoji Temple

Mt. Daigo 450 ▲

Hokaiji Temple

Kanshuji Temple

Fushimi-Momoyama Castle

FUSHIMI

ROKUJIZO

KOHATA

OBAKU

Mampukuji Temple

KEIHAN-UJI

Mimurotoji Temple

Byodoin Temple

UJI

Uji R.

(24)

KINTETSU RY.

TO NARA

TO KINTETSU-NARA

TANBABASHI

MOMOYAMA

CHUSHOJIMA

ODO

YODO

KEIHAN RY.

Katsura R.

Kinugawa R.

HIGASHI-MUKO

MUKOMACHI

KOTARI

NAGAOKA-TENJIN

HANKYU RY.

TOKAIDO MAIN LINE

TOKAIDO SHINKANSEN

YAMAZAKI

TO OSAKA

KYOTO MINAMI I.C.

(1)

(171)

ALL ABOUT KYOTO

KYOTO TODAY

Kyoto has always been Japan's best-known tourist attraction and, without doubt, if there is one city in Japan that the foreign visitor should see, it is Kyoto.

For Japanese, it is the "heart of the country", a position that accurately reflects its important role in Japanese history, culture and sentiment. Today, though Kyoto is part of modern-day Japan, so much tradition survives here that this ancient center of Buddhism seems to be a place apart from the busy world. Scattered around the city are numerous tranquil, beautiful sites that exemplify the best in Japanese tradition. These include two magnificent Imperial Villas, 400 Shintō shrines and 1,650 Buddhist temples—rich in history, unique architectural beauty and art treasures—as well as over 60 exquisite temple gardens. It is also a city of festivals, with many centuries-old fetes filling its calendar.

Moreover, as a tourist city, Kyoto offers all the modern facilities necessary for visitors to enjoy their stay and to appreciate the city's beauty, explore its history, or simply relax in restful surroundings.

LOCATION

Kyoto Prefecture lies in the north of the Kinki Region, almost in the center of Japan's chain of islands. The prefecture faces the Japan Sea in the north and stretches southeast, covering the mountain areas of Tamba, Tango, Daigo and Kasagi.

Kyoto City is the prefectural capital and an important junction for transportation in the region. It lies in a basin in the southeast of Kyoto Prefecture, surrounded by low mountains, which include Mt. Hiei, Mt. Kurama and Higashiyama. In ancient times, these mountains served to protect Kyoto from surrounding enemies and allowed the city to prosper as the country's political and cultural center.

AREA & POPULATION

Kyoto Prefecture consists of 11 cities and 33 towns and covers an area of 4,613 sq.km. Of this area, Kyoto City occupies 611 sq.km. It lies between Latitude 34°52′N and 34°19′N and in Longitude, extends from 135°36′E to 135°53′E. Kyoto city is divided into 11 administrative wards with a total population of 1,479,000, making it the 6th largest city in the nation. Kyoto has a sister-city relationship with Paris, Boston, Cologne, Florence, Kiev, Xian, Guadalajara and Zagreb.

Kyoto is divided into 5 sections: Rakuchū in the center, Higashiyama in the east, Rakuhoku in the north, Rakusai in the west, and Rakunan in the south.

CLIMATE

Kyoto lies in a shallow basin, surrounded by mountains which impede convection and trap warm air in summer and cold air in winter. Thus, summers in Kyoto are rather sultry, with tempertures reaching over 30°C in August. Even at night, temperatures remain high. Winters, on the other hand are very cold, although, with generally dry winds there is little snow. The fine, mild weather in spring and autumn makes these seasons the best time to visit Kyoto.

21

Average figures from 1951 to 1980

Monthly Average Temperature in Kyoto (°C)												
JAN.	FEB.	MAR.	APR.	MAY	JUN.	JUL.	AUG.	SEP.	OCT.	NOV.	DEC.	ANN.
3.9	4.6	7.6	13.7	18.4	22.1	26.3	27.5	23.2	17.0	11.4	6.4	15.2

Monthly Average Humidity in Kyoto (%)												
JAN.	FEB.	MAR.	APR.	MAY	JUN.	JUL.	AUG.	SEP.	OCT.	NOV.	DEC.	ANN.
71	70	66	65	66	72	74	71	73	72	72	72	70

Monthly Average Rainfall in Kyoto (mm)												
JAN.	FEB.	MAR.	APR.	MAY	JUN.	JUL.	AUG.	SEP.	OCT.	NOV.	DEC.	ANN.
57	67	108	163	156	247	250	176	206	118	75	45	1669

PEOPLE

Modernization has crept over Kyoto and a lot of old customs and conventions have naturally disappeared. However, the basic nature of the people in this great city has not changed. Kyotoites remain proud of their refined culture, lifestyle and dialect, and this pride manifests itself in a respect for tradition and an attachment to the past. The large number of festivals in Kyoto and the enthusiasm in which they are celebrated is testimony of this respect for tradition—and of the care taken to preserve the best of their inheritance. Kyoto still thrives as the center of traditional arts and crafts, while at the same time being a modern city and an important industrial center. Kyotoites have succeeded in preserving and fostering tradition and in blending it with a modern world. Kyotoites are justifiably proud—but never boastful—and visitors will find a warm, gentle and courteous people welcoming them.

FLOWER CALENDAR

Late February : Japanese Apricot Blossoms Kitano Temmangū Shrine, Kyoto Imperial Park, Zuishin-in Temple
Late March to late April : Cherry Blossoms Kyoto Imperial Park, Nijō Castle, Tetsugaku-no-Michi Path, Arashiyama Hill, Maruyama Park, Heian Shrine, Nin-naji Temple, Kiyomizu Temple, Shōjiji Temple, Daikakuji Temple, Daigoji Temple
Late April to mid-June : Azaleas Shōren-in Temple, Manshuin Temple, Shisendō hermitage, Banks of the Hozu River, Shōdenji Temple
Late May to mid-June : Wisteria, Irises Byōdōin Temple, Heian Shrine, Shisendō hermitage
Early June : Hydrangea Shisendō hermitage, Sanzen-in Temple
Late September : Bush Clover Nanzenji Temple, Heian Shrine
October to November : Chrysanthemum Arashiyama, Daikakuji Temple, Fushimi Momoyama Castle, Botanical Gardens
Early November : Autumnal Leaves Kiyomizu Temple, Eikandō Tōfukuji Temple, Ōhara, Sambi, Sagano, Kurama, Nanzenji Temple

HISTORY

Japan was first inhabited in the later Stone Age during the Neolithic Period and evidence of a primitive culture from this time, including earthenware and other relics, has been excavated in Kyoto. There were three distinct periods of primitive culture before the 4th C when family groups were loosely united into a state, centered around the *Yamato* court in the present Nara Prefecture. Culture from Korea and China flowed into the country, including Confucianism, Buddhism, the Chinese writing system and literature. The *Nara era* (710-794) followed and was a time of great prosperity. The wealth and power of Buddhist temples grew to such an extent that they posed a threat to the ruler and Emperor *Kammu* moved the capital to *Heian-kyō* (now Kyoto) in 794.

At the start of the *Heian era* (794-1192), Kyoto was laid out in a checkerboard pattern, following the design of Chinese cities. Also at this time the *Fujiwara* family, which was related to the Imperial family, gained political power and held important positions in government. They neglected administration and corruption grew until civil war broke out and the authority of the *Fujiwara* clan was replaced by the rule of the *Heishi* family. They repeated the excesses of their predecessors but regime was short-lived. In 1185, they were overthrown by their old enemies, the *Genji* clan, in a battle at *Dannoura* (Shimonoseki). This led to the *Kamakura era* (1192-1333).

The *Minamoto* family (part of the *Genji* clan) and their advisers, the *Hōjō* family, ruled the nation from their headquarters in Kamakura and formed a military government under control of a *shōgun*. During this time, Kyoto developed as a commercial and manufacturing city. In the period of unrest following the repulsion of a Mongol invasion, Emperor *Godaigo* regained power briefly for the Imperial throne. However, he failed to reward his military commanders and indulged his courtiers, so forces under the *Ashikaga* samurai family drove him out. They established a new military government, the *Muromachi Shogunate*, in 1336. The period from

23

1336 to 1573 is known as the *Muromachi era*.

The luxury of Kyoto life led to poor administration, heavy taxes and after succession problems with the Shogunate, a civil war (1467-1477). During the war, fires swept over the city, provoking the peasants and Buddhist priests into frequent rioting against the Shogunate. The shaky government was taken over in 1573 by the feudal lord *Nobunaga Oda*. However, he was assassinated in 1582 and in the struggle to unite the feudal lords and control the country, *Hideyoshi Toyotomi* triumphed. He built the mighty Osaka Castle and also constructed a fortress in Kyoto, designed to control the entire city. He also ordered the construction of numerous

C	Era		Japan(kyoto)	World	
	Asuka Era	538	Introduction of Buddhism to Japan	610	Islam Founded by Mahomet
		645	Taika Reform	618	T'ang Dynasty established
		667	Capital moved to Otsu-kyo(Shiga)		
	Nara Era	710	Capital moved to Heijō-Kyō (Nara)		
		784	Capital moved to Nagaoka-kyo(province of Kyōto)		
		788	Enryakuji Temple built		
		794	Capital moved to Heian-kyō (central Kyoto)		
		798	Kiyomizu Temple built		
		805	Kurama Temple built	829	Unification of England
		874	Daigoji Temple built		
		876	Daikakuji Temple built		
	Heian Era	1052	Byōdōin Temple built	1066	Norman Conquest (William the Conquerer)
		1156	Hogen-no-ran (Civil War)		
		1159	Heiji-no-ran (Civil War)		
		1164	Sanjūsangendō built	1096	First Crusade
		1185	Heishi Clan annihilated in the Battle of Dannoura		
	Kamakura Era	1192	Kamakura Shogunate established by Minamoto-no-Yoritomo		
		1221	Jōkyū-no-ran (rebellion)	1272	Marco Polo travelled through Asia

temples and generally attempted to revive the city.

Ieyasu Tokugawa succeeded *Toyotomi* and the *Edo* (or *Tokugawa*) *era* followed. He set up a military government in Edo (now Tokyo), while the Emperor, who had no substantial power, remained in Kyoto. During the *Edo era* (1603-1867), Kyoto flourished as a center of religion and learning and this period saw industry and art thrive. Strict military control of the country lasted nearly 300 years, until the restoration of Emperor Meiji in 1868. The period that followed, known as the *Meiji era* (1868-1912), saw the birth of modern Japan, and the transformation from an isolated feudal country into one of the world's most powerful and dynamic nations.

C	Era		Japan(Kyoto)		World
	Nambokucho Era	1333	Kamakura Shogunate fell		
		1336	Muromachi Shogunate established		
	Muromachi Era	1467	Ōnin-no-ran (Civil War)	1492	Columbus discovered American Continent
		1573	Muromachi Shogunate fell	1522	Magellan circled the globe
	AzuchiMo-moyama Era	1600	Battle of Sekigahara		
	Edo Era	1603	Ieyasu Tokugawa established Edo Shogunate		
		1613	Prohibition of Christian belief	1620	British Pilgrims departed for New World in Mayflower
		1639	Japan closed to the outside world.	1649	Cromwell established republic in England
				1660	English Restoration
				1776	Declaration of Independence of U.S.A.
		1853	Perry arrived at Uraga	1861	American Civil War began
	Meiji Era	1868	Meiji Restoration		
		1869	Tokyo became the capital of Japan		

*Taishō era (1912~1926), Shōwa era (1926~1989) and Heisei era (1989~) follow the above history.

25

GETTING AROUND KYOTO

GETTING TO KYOTO

● **RAILWAYS**

Tokyo to Kyoto: 2hrs. 15min. by JR Shinkansen Line, Osaka to Kyoto: 30min. by JR.

Nagoya to Kyoto: 35min. by JR Shinkansen Line.

Umeda (Osaka) to Kawaramachi (Kyoto): 40min. by Hankyū Electric Railway.

Yodoyabashi (Osaka) to Sanjo (Kyoto): 45min. by Keihan Railway.

● **BUSES**

Tokyo to Kyoto 8hr. by JR Highway bus.

● **EXPRESSWAYS**

Tokyo to Kyoto: 490km. on the Tōmei (Tokyo-Nagoya) and Meishin (Nagoya-Kobe) Expressways.

Nishinomiya (Kobe) to Kyoto: 50km. on the Meishin Expressway.

● **AIRLINES**

Haneda (Tokyo) to Itami (Osaka): 1hr. by JAL, ANA or JAS ; 1hr. by Ariport Limousine to the center of Kyoto.

● **JAPAN RAIL PASS**

This pass is valid for the entire network of JR lines, including the Shinkansen, and is available only to foreign tourists visiting Japan for sightseeing purposes. To obtain the pass, an Exchange Voucher must be purchased outside of Japan. They are available at JTB (Japan Travel Bureau) overseas offices or other authorized travel agencies in major cities throughout the world. After arriving in Japan, the pass can be obtained by turning in the Exchange Voucher at JR ticket offices. Seat reservations may be made at no extra cost. There are two types of pass: Green (1st Class) and Ordinary (Economy).

TRANSPORTATION IN KYOTO

Kyoto Prefecture's sightseeing attractions are centered around Kyoto City. Taxis and the subway and bus lines radiating from Kyoto Station will get visitors to most attractions in the city. However, trains are necessary for visiting temples and shrines in outlying areas.

● *BUSES*

There are nearly 100 interconnecting routes in Kyoto, with buses run by the following lines: City Bus, Kyoto Bus, Keihan Bus, Kyoto Kōtsū, JR Bus and Hankyū Bus, Major terminals include Kyoto Station, Sanjō-Keihan, Shijō-Kawaramachi, Shijō-Karasuma, Shijō-Ōmiya and Kitaōji Bus Terminal (above Kitaōji subway station). There is a standard fare of ¥200. One-day "Free Passes" are available.

● *RAILWAYS*

Subway: A line extends directly north from Takeda Station through Kyoto Station to Kitayama Station.

Hankyū Electric Railway (Kyoto Line): heads southwest to Nishiyama beneath Shijō dori Street and stops at Kawaramachi, Karasuma and Hankyū-Ōmiya.

Keifuku Electric Railway (Arashiyama Line): runs westward from Shijō-Ōmiya (near Nijō Castle) to Arashiyama.

Eizan Electric Railway: runs to Kurama-Kibune and Yase in the northeast of the city.

Keihan Electric Railway: a line connects Higashiyama in the east with Rakunan and Uji in the south.

Kinki Nippon Railway (Kintetsu): a line runs from Kyoto Station to Nara and Osaka.

JR: The Tōkaidō Line traverses Kyoto from Shiga Prefecture to Osaka; the San-in Line extends west to Sagano and Arashiyama; the Nara Line runs from Kyoto Station to Nara via Uji.

● *TAXIS AND RENTAL CARS*

Taxis are an ideal way of travelling between attractions and can be hailed. Charter taxis with guides are available for hire. Rental cars are suitable for travelling to rural areas such as

Mt. Hiei and Nishiyama but battling the traffic in the central city is not recommended.

● **RENT-A-CYCLE**

Cycles are popular for visiting temples in Ōhara, Arashiyama and Sagano. Cycles can be hired for a half or full day at a rate of between ¥800—¥1,300 per day.

● **CABLE CARS AND ROPEWAYS**

A cable car runs from Yase Amusement Park to the foot of Mt. Hiei and a ropeway takes visitor to the summit.

MODEL COURSES

Organized sightseeing tours offered by travel companies are an efficient means of sightseeing for visitors with limited time. However, carefully planned courses can often be more enjoyable even in an unknown city, since they allow more freedom and provide a little adventure. The model courses introduced here can be used as guides in planning your routes.

Key:═══Bus — on foot▬▬▬JR Railway++++++Private Railway

● **LEISURELY 5-DAY ROUND TRIP**

Day 1: A stroll around Sagano and Arashiyama.

Kyoto Station═══Tōji Temple═══Kōryūji Temple ═══Sagano, Arashiyama═══Sambi **Day 2:** Rakusai and Rakuhoku (east and north). Nin-naji Temple —— Ryōanji Temple ═══ Kinkakuji Temple ═══ Kōetsuji Temple ═══Daitokuji Temple═══Kamigamo Shrine **Day 3:** A leisurely walk along Tetsugaku-no-michi Path. (From Ginkakuji to Nanzenji Temple) Ōhara═══Shisendō hermitage ═══Ginkakuji Temple —— Nanzenji Temple —— Heian Shrine **Day 4:** From Rakuchū to Rakunan (moving south). Yasaka Shrine —— San-nen-zaka Hill and Ninen-zaka Hill —— Kiyomizu Temple ═══ Sanjūsangendō ═══ Sen-nyūji Temple —— Tōfukuji Temple═══Fushimi Inari Shrine **Day 5:** Uji Area. Mampukuji Temple++++++Byōdōin Temple▬▬▬ Kyoto Station.

● QUICK TOUR

A course covering selected highlights. **Day 1:** Kyoto Station
—— Nishi-Honganji Temple —— Higashi-Honganji Temple
=====Sanjūsangendō=====Kiyomizu Temple=====Heian
Shrine —— Nanzenji Temple —— Ginkakuji Temple.
Day 2: Nijō Castle=====Kinkakuji Temple=====Ryōanji
Temple =====Nin-naji Temple ++++++++ Sagano, Arashiyama
=====Kyoto Station.

● ONE DAY COURSES

Higashiyama Course (Buddhist art, architecture, Japanese gardens)
Kyoto Station=====Sanjūsangendō=====Kiyomizu Temple —— Yasaka Shrine —— Chion-in Temple —— Heian Shrine=====Higashi-Honganji Temple.

Rakuhoku Course (Attractions around Horikawa Street in central Kyoto)
Kyoto Station —— Higashi-Honganji Temple —— Nishi-Honganji Temple=====Nijō Castle=====Shōdenji Temple =====Daitokuji Temple=====Kamigamo Shrine.

Rakusai Course (Strolling and sightseeing in the Sagano and Arashiyama Hill areas)
Kyoto Station===== Kōryūji Temple —— Movie Village ===== Sagano, Arashiyama Hill ===== Kinkakuji Temple =====Nishi-Honganji temple.

29

RAKUCHU

500m

TO SHOKOKUJI TEMPLE

SHIMOGAMO SHRINE

DEMACHI YANAGI

Kamo-Ohashi Bridge

Prefectural Hospital
FURITSU-DAIBYOIN-MAE

Rozanji Temple

KAWABATA-DORI ST.

Kyoto Univ. Hospital

HIGASHI-OJI-DORI ST.

Kyoto Handicraft Center

Heian Shrine

OKAZAKI

Nijo-Ohashi Kyoto Municipal Museum
Bridge of Traditional Industry

National Museum of Modern Art

Shoren-in Temple

TO HAMAOTSU

KEIHAN RY. KYOZU LINE

Chion-in Temple

CHIONIN-MAE

HIGASHIYAMA-SANJO

SANJO

Sanjo-Ohashi Bridge

SHIN-KYOGOKU

TO KAMIGAMO SHRINE

Doshisha Univ.

IMADEGAWA

KARASUMA-IMADEGAWA

Kyoto Imperial Palace

Omiya Palace

Sento Palace

Kyoto Imperial Park

DOSHISHA-MAE

SUBWAY KARASUMA LINE

MARUTAMACHI

KAWARAMACHI-DORI ST.

Gyoganji(Kodo) Temple

Hotel Fujita Kyoto

City Office

NIJO-DORI ST.

OIKE-DORI ST.

OIKE

Honnoji Temple

Heian Museum of Ancient History

KARASUMA-SANJO

Rokkakudo Temple

TO KAMIGAMO SHRINE

HORIKAWA-IMADEGAWA

Toraya Kurokawa

Kyoto Prefectural Office

Kyoto Palace-Side Hotel

Fuka

MARUTAMACHI-DORI ST.

Matsumaeya

Kyoto International Hotel

NIJOJO-MAE

SUBWAY KARASUMA LINE

SHIBAKO-MAE

MARUTAMACHI

Kitano-Temmangu Shrine

IMADEGAWA-DORI ST.

Tsuruya Yoshinobu

Nishijin Textile Center

NISHIJIN

ICHIJO-DORI ST.

Mankamero

Juttoku

SENBON-DORI ST.

Nijo Castle

Shinzen-en Garden

SHINZENEN-MAE

Nijo Jinya

SANJO-DORI ST.

NIJO

KITANO-TEMMANGU-MAE

Horinji Temple

TO SAGA
SANIN MAIN LINE

NISHINOKYO

RAKUCHU

Rakuchū is the central urban district of Kyoto city and its name dates from the 16th C when Hideyoshi Toyotomi (1536 –1598) ordered an earthwork defence to be built around the city. The area inside the earthwork was called Rakuchū and the area outside, Rakugai. Today only the name is left as a reminder of these former defences and the Rakuchū district is no longer so clearly defined. Although present day Rakuchū is a progressive modern district, much of its history has been preserved and the flavor of the old city is being consciously protected.

KYOTO STATION

Kyoto Station is centrally located and serves as a gateway to the city. The area around the station is rich in places of historical interest.

WHAT TO SEE

● **KYOTO TOWER** Directly in front of the station is this imposing candle-shaped observation tower atop the Kyoto Tower Building. It has an observation deck 100m up which provides fine views over the city.

● **HIGASHI-HONGANJI TEMPLE** This magnificent temple is the headquarters of the *Ōtani* school of the *Jōdo-shinshū* sect. It was founded by the first Edo-era *shōgun, Ieyasu Tokugawa*(1542—1616) in 1602 as a rival to Nishi Hongan-ji. The original structures were repeatedly destroyed by fire and the present buildings, some of the finest examples of Japanese Buddhist architecture, date from 1895. 5 min. walk north of Kyoto Station.

Daishidō(Founder's Hall) This enormous, elaborately decorated double-roofed hall contains a statue of Priest *Shinran* (1173-1262), founder of the sect, reputedly carved by the saint himself. Over 50 ropes, made from hair donated by female devotees, are displayed inside. They were used to haul the giant logs used in the building's construction.

Hondō (Main Hall) This hall stands to the south of Dai-

Higashi Honganji Temple

shidō and is connected with it by a corridor. It houses an image of *Amida-Nyorai* attributed to *Kaikei*, a renowned sculptor of the early 13th C.

Daishidōmon Gate Often called *Daimon*, this magnificently decorated 2-storied gate is 27m high with an *Irimoya*-style roof.

Shōsei Garden This beautiful garden, celebrated in poetry, is to the east of the temple and was completed in 1657. It is landscaped in the go-round style with various buildings arranged around *Ingetsu* Pond in the center.

● **NISHI-HONGANJI TEMPLE**

Nishi Hongan-ji is the main temple of the *Jōdo-shinshū* sect. Originally founded in 1272 at Higashiyama, it was moved to its present site in 1591, when land was provided by *Hideyoshi Toyotomi*. To the west of Higasi-Honganji Temple.

Goeidō (Founder's Hall) An "Important Cultural property", this great hall was rebuilt in 1636 and contains a statue of the founder, carved by *Shinran* himself at the age of 71. The gate in front of the hall is regarded as the finest of its kind in Kyoto.

Hondō (Main Hall) This elaborately decorated hall was rebuilt in 1760. The interior features splendid sliding screens, painted with phoenixes and peacocks.

Daishoin Hall This is the largest *Shoinzukuri* building remaining. *Shoinzukuri* construction, developed in the Muromachi era (14th C—16th C), features buildings centered around the *Shoin* — a large room used for ceremonies and entertaining guests.

33

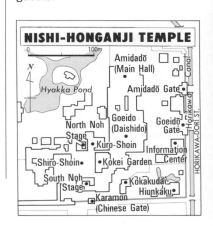

Hiunkaku Pavilion This unique 3-story building combines 3 different architectural styles and contains *Hideyoshi Toyotomi's* tearooms, a bathroom and a rest chamber. It is decorated throughout with paintings by master artists of the *Kanō* school. Closed to the public.

Karamon (Chinese Gate) This gate features brilliantly-colored carvings and metalwork. It is also known as *Higurashimon* (Sunset Gate), the implication being that while totally absorbed in admiring its beauty one can fail to notice that the sun has set.

● ***SHIMABARA*** In its heyday, Shimabara was one of Japan's foremost pleasure quarters. Only two buildings in this area still retain an Edo-era atmosphere. A large gate marks the entrance to the quarter. Get off the bus at Shimabara-guchi.

● ***SUMIYA*** Masterpiece of the *ageya* architectural style, designated as a National Cultural Treasure. An *ageya*, representing typical Edo-era merchant culture, was an elegant restaurant where banquets and dinner parties were held. The 2-story building roofed with tiles, copper plates and shingles has 3 main parts: the lattice work exterior and entry way, the huge, open kitchen, and the interior rooms. It functioned as a meeting place and cultural salon where famous artists, writers, politicians, etc. gathered. Get off the bus at Shimabara-guchi and walk 6 min. west.

● ***TOJI TEMPLE*** This is the *Tōji* branch headquarters of the *Shingon* Buddhist sect and boasts some of the largest temple buildings erected in the Momoyama era. Founded in 796 by imperial order, it was given in 823 to priest *Kūkai* (774 — 835), *founder of the Shingon* sect, also known by his posthumous title of *Kōbō-Daishi*. Tōji eventually developed into the chief Buddhist temple in Japan. Get off the bus at the east gate.

Nandaimon Gate This is the main gate of Tōji Temple. The original burnt down and

Shimabara

the present one was moved from in front of Sanjūsangen-dō in 1894.

Gojū-no-tō (Five-storied Pagoda) This pagoda, the tallest in Japan at 55m, was rebuilt in 1644 and has come to be emblematic of Kyoto.

Kondō (Main Hall) Rebuilt in 1606, this hall is a masterpiece of Momoyama era Buddhist architecture and one of the largest of its kind. It is constructed in a skilful combination of Japanese, Chinese and Indian styles.

Kōdō (Lecture Hall) Originally built by *Kūkai* in 825 as a seminary for Tantric Buddhism, this hall was rebuilt in the 17th C.

WHAT TO BUY

For last-minute shopping, Kyoto Station's underground shopping arcade **Porta** contains a large number of souvenir stores selling traditonal Kyoto goods. **Nakayama** sells Kyoto dolls and **Jūsanya** is well-known for its excellent hand-made boxwood shoes. **Kyōsendō** sells colorful, high-quality folding fans. **Mametomi-hompo** in front of the station, is famous for its five colored beans. Near the south exit, the **Avanti** building contains stores selling souvenirs.

SHIJO & NIJO CASTLE

The central area bounded by Shijō, Sanjō and Kawaramachi streets was originally Kyoto's artistic and cultural center and is now a bustling, lively shopping district with many department stores, banks and restaurants. In contrast, the area around Nijō Castle is quiet with many spots of cultural and historical interest.

WHAT TO SEE

● **MIBUDERA TEMPLE** Founded in 991, this temple of the *Risshū* sect was rebuilt in 1970 and is famous for its *Kyōgen* performance which teaches Buddhist doctrine through pantomime, held from April 21-29 every year. Shijōbōjō bus stop. walk 3min. south.

● **KODAI YUZEN-EN** Kodai-Yūzen-en is a building devoted to *Yūzen* dyeing, a traditional Kyoto art. It houses the Yūzen Art Museum with paintings, scrolls and period clothing all exhibiting the dyeing method perfected by the 17th C Kyoto painter *Yūzen Miyazaki*. There are also displays of dyeing patterns and tools, a kiosk selling dyed goods and a movie explaining the dyeing process. Get off the bus at Horikawa

35

Matsubara and walk 5min. northwest.

● **SHIJO STREET** Constructed in the Heian era (8th C—12th C), this broad, bustling thoroughfare runs east to west through the heart of the city. Once the artistic and cultural center, it is now a busy shopping area with shops, banks, restaurants and department stores including **Daimaru**, **Fujii-Daimaru**, **Hankyū** and **Takashimaya**. The Kyoto Line of the Hankyū Electric Railway runs under the street, starting in Kawara-machi and ending at Umeda in Osaka. The Keifuku Electric Railway runs from Shijō-

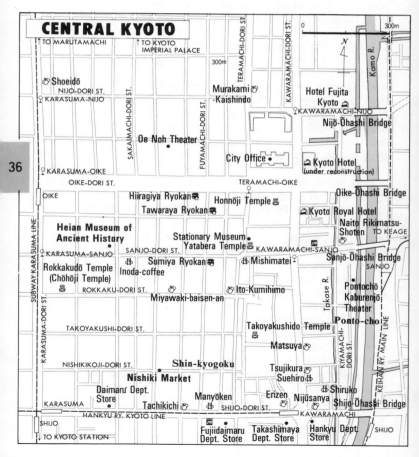

CENTRAL KYOTO

Ōmiya, the west side of Shijō-Street, to scenic Arashiyama in the northwestern suburbs. Get off the bus at Shijō-Kawaramachi.

● **SHIN-KYŌGOKU** Better known to foreign tourists as **Theater Street**, this is a popular arcade lined with theaters, cinemas, restaurants and souvenir shops. The street extends north from about the center of Shijō Street, between Kawaramachi and Karasuma, to Sanjō Street and the entrances to a number of temples lead directly off it. Get off the bus at Kawaramachi-Sanjō or Shijō-Kawaramachi.

● **PONTO-CHO** Located east of Shin-Kyōgoku, sandwiched between the Kamo River and Takase Canal, Ponto-Chō ranks with Gion as one of Kyoto's best-known entertainment districts. Once a red-light district, it has alleys full of restaurants and bars as well as teahouses for *geisha* entertainment. The **Kaburen-jō Theater** here is famous for its *Kamogawa-Odori* Dance, held annually from May 1 to 24 and Oct. 15 to Nov. 7. These dances and dance dramas are performed by *geisha* accompanied by traditional music. Get off the bus at Shijō-Kawaramachi or

Nijō Castle

Kawaramachi-Sanjō and walk 3min. east.

● **HEIAN MUSEUM OF ANCIENT HISTORY** Located on Sanjō Street in a western style building that was formerly the Bank of Japan, this museum displays articles dating from primitive times to the Heian era that have been excavated from historical sites in the Kyoto region. Get off the bus at Karasuma-Sanjō and walk 3min. east.

● **NIJO CASTLE** Nijō Castle was built in 1603 by *Ieyasu Tokugawa* and served as his residence when he visited Kyoto from Edo (now Tokyo). After the Meiji Restoration in 1868 when the Tokugawa shogunate was overthrown, Nijō Castle became a detached palace for the Imperial House. Later, in 1939, it was given to the Kyoto municipality. Its

37

buildings are national treasures — with splendid architectural beauty and richly decorated interiors. Get off the bus in front of the castle.

Karamon (Chinese Gate) A cultural treasure of the Momoyama era, this gate is decorated with beautiful wooden carvings and exquisite metalwork and once formed part of Hideyoshi's Fushimi Castle.

Tozamurai (First Building) The largest structure in the Castle, this building comprises numerous profusely decorated chambers including the *Chokushi-no-ma* (Imperial Messenger's Chamber) with beautiful carvings on its shelves and cabinets and impressive paintings on the sliding screens.

Ōhiroma (Third Building) This consists of the Great Hall and 4 other chambers. The Great Hall was used by the *Shōgun* when holding audiences with his *daimyō* (local lords). The shelves and cabinets are richly decorated while the sliding doors are covered largely with paintings of pine trees. Each room has a different colored pattern on its coffered ceiling.

Uguisubari-no-rōka (Nightingale Corridor) This corri-

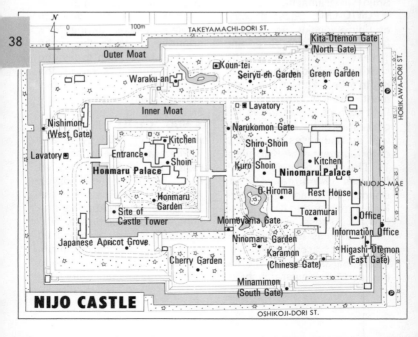

NIJO CASTLE

dor, which leads from the entrance to the Ōhiroma, has a squeaky floor designed to warn of the approach of possible enemies. The floorboards give out a noise not unlike the sound of the *uguisu*, a Japanese warbler, often dubbed nightingale for its song.

Ni-no-Maru Garden This meticulously designed garden originally contained no trees, as falling leaves were considered a reminder of the transitoriness of life. In later years cherry, maple, pine and other trees were added to enhance the garden's beauty. It is laid out in the go-round style with a center pond with three islets spanned by stone bridges.

WHAT TO BUY

● **NIJUSANYA** Located on Shijō Street, this is a specialist comb shop founded in the Edo era. Its high quality boxwood combs, in a variety of styles, are true works of art.

●**TACHIKICHI** Established in 1752, this famous store sells a wide range of quality ceramic goods.

● **MORITA WASHI** This Japanese paper wholesale store also has a retail outlet next door. Here they make over 3,000 varieties of the

Miyawaki Baisen-an

well-known paper called *Kyōchiyogami* with its traditional delicate shades. In addition they supply the country with numerous other types of paper and traditional paper products including fascinating small boxes, dolls and miniclosets.

● **MIYAWAKI BAINEN-AN** Established in 1823, this store stocks a vast assortment of folding fans for which Kyoto is famous. They include those used in dances and tea ceremonies and a variety of ornamental fans. The shop building itself is impressive, with its conspicuous *bengara* (scarlet colored) latticework facade.

● **TSUJIKURA** This shop is overflowing with umbrellas and lanterns with an amazing selection of colors and

39

designs. Here you'll find *ban-gasa* (paper umbrellas) and *Janome-gasa* (oil paper umbrellas decorated with Bull's-eye designs) as well as those used in Japanese dances.

● **NAITO RIKIMATSU SHOTEN** This novelty shop has been selling hemp-palm brooms and brushes since the Edo era. There is everything from brushes for cleaning false teeth to yard brooms.

● **ERIZEN** Erizen sells kimono of the finest quality, dealing largely with *Nishijin* and *Yūzen* dyed fabrics and stocking many original designs.

● **MATSUYA** This doll shop dates from the early Edo era and specializes in *Hina* dolls (for Girl's Day) *Musha* dolls (warrior dolls for Boy's Day) as well as *Gosho* (palace) dolls. Often dressed in Nishi-jin garments, the dolls are superb works of art and some cost up to one million yen.

● **ITO KUMIHIMO-TEN** This shop has sold plaited cord for over 150 years. There are cords for Kimono, *haori* (half-coats), decorative varieties for use in art work and they can also be made to order.

● **SHOEIDŌ** Located on Kara-suma Street, this store has been a leading supplier of incense for over 280 years. There are over 300 varieties to choose from and recommended for souvenirs are *hanakuruma* — incense bags made from delicate *chiyogami* paper.

WHERE TO EAT

● **MAN-YOKEN** A trail blazer among high-class Western style restaurants in Kyoto, Man-yōken serves authentic

---

NISHIKI MARKET

North of Shijō Dōri is a small lane running east-west for about 400m. This is Nishiki-kōji and here you can find a market with numerous fresh food shops selling such items as fish, freshly made gluten wheat bread, dried bean curd and *tsukemono* (pickled vegetables). This market started in the Momoyama era and is still thriving today. It is always a bustling and lively area, filled with local people and tourists and is an excellent place to savor some of the local atmosphere.

French cuisine in a grand building with Louis XIV furnishings.

● *TOKASAIKAN* Serving Peking dishes in the style of the Imperial Court cuisine of old China, this famous restaurant is housed in an equally majestic building. The atmosphere, however, remains friendly and relaxed and in summer a beer garden overlooking the Kamo River is opened.

● *SHIRUKO* The main attractions here are *Miso soup* and the renowned *Rikyū bentō* (boxed lunches) — veritable works of art.

● *SUEHIRO* This restaurant raises its own livestock to ensure the highest quality beef for its superb *shabu-shabu* (pot boiled dish), stews and steaks.

● *MISHIMATEI* Kyoto's preeminent *sukiyaki* restaurant. The taste and quality of its beef and the appealing decor contribute to its outstanding reputation.

● *INODA COFFEE* It is said "Morning in Kyoto is Inoda", a tribute to the reputation of this artistic shop with its lavish interior and sumptuous living room atmosphere.

● *MURAKAMI KAISHINDO* Delicious cakes are available here, including the unusual and superlative *Kōzubukuro*

Nishiki Market

— a cake with a center of mandarin orange juice set in gelatin.

NIGHT LIFE

For a peaceful drink while admiring the city lights the **Starlight Bar** on the top floor of the Kyoto International Hotel is tops. The Hotel Fujita's **Ishimizu Bar** has an adult atmosphere along with a Japanese garden and live music. Other places of note along Kiyamachi Street include the Jazz coffee shops **Bluenote** and **Lady Day**.

KYOTO IMPERIAL PALACE

The area around the Imperial Palace features many old temples and shrines. Moving across the river from there you come to the Tadasu-no-mori and Nishijin areas, both districts which flourished dur-

41

ing the Heian era.

● *KYOTO IMPERIAL PALACE*
Originally built as the Emperor's second palace, the Kyoto Imperial Palace complex (*Kyoto Gosho*) was used as the Imperial palace from 1331 to 1867 after the original main palace burnt down. During that time a court town under the control of the *shō-gun* was built. The Palace consists of numerous large wooden buildings constructed in the *Shinden* style. In this style, popular for residences of the nobility during the Heian era, all the buildings are connected by a covered gallery.

Shishinden (Ceremonial Hall) This hall is the main palace of the complex and is also known as **Nanden**(South Palace). It consists of a single-story building in the *Irimoya* style, and is thatched with cypress bark. It was used for important state functions such as the enthronement of the Emperor and the New Year's audience. The hall contains a throne called *Takamikura*, covered with rich silk cloth, and on each side of it are stands intended for the Sacred Treasures (swords and jewels). The sliding

screens here exhibit paintings by *Hiroyuki Sumiyoshi* of the Twenty-two Chinese sages, replicas of the originals created in 888 by *Kanaoka Kose*, a painter of the late 9th C.

Seiryōden Hall This hall is partioned into several chambers, the main one containing a matted dais, covered with a silk canopy, where the Emperor sat on formal occasions. At the sides of the dais are stands for the Imperial Regalia and at the sides of the dais steps are two wooden *Komainu* — mythical animals believed to ward off evil

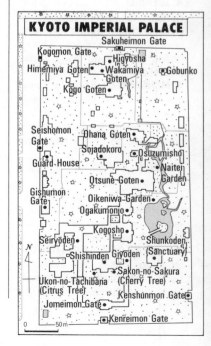

KYOTO IMPERIAL PALACE

Sakuheimon Gate
Kogomon Gate
Higyōsha
Himemiya Goten • Wakamiya • Gobunko
Goten
Kōgo Goten •
Seishomon Gate
Ōhana Goten •
Sojadokoro
Osuzumisho
Guard House
Naiteı Garden
Otsune Goten •
Gishumon Gate
Oikeniwa Garden •
Ogakumonjo •
Kogosho •
Seiryōden •
Shunkoden (Sanctuary)
Shishinden Giyōden
Sakon-no-Sakura (Cherry Tree)
Ukon-no-Tachibana (Citrus Tree)
Kenshunmon Gate
Jomeimon Gate •
Kenreimon Gate

N

0 — 50 m

spirits. The sliding screens are decorated with paintings of the *Tosa* school, each one accompanied by a Chinese or Japanese poem. The hall was originally used as living quarters for the Emperor but was later set aside for ceremonial use only. For large group visits to the Imperial Household Agency advance permission is required. Enquiries can be made at travel agencies. Get off the bus at Karasuma Ichijō.

● *SENTŌ GOSHO* Located on the southeast side of the Imperial Palace, this is the site of a palace built in 1629 for the retired Emperor Gomizuno-o. The palace was destroyed by fire in 1854 and the garden in which it stood contains two ponds and 8 small shrines. The rocks and grove of old trees here convey a mysterious atmosphere of enchantment. Get off the bus at Karasuma Shimo-chōja-machi.

● *ROZANJI TEMPLE* Located to the east of Kyoto Gyoen Park, this temple is within the Imperial Palace complex and contains many tombs of the Imperial family. The temple's main hall was transferred from Sentō palace, as a token of the Imperial family's devotion. Genji Park is also in this

Kyoto Imperial Palace

vicinity and is named after the *Tale of Genji*, written by *Murasaki Shikibu*, since the remains of her mansion are located here. Get off the bus at Furitsu Idai Byōin-mae.

● *SHŌKOKUJI TEMPLE* Located in an ancient pine grove on the north side of Dōshisha University, this temple was erected by Imperial order in 1392. The original buildings were almost totally destroyed by fire during the civil wars of the 15th C. It was rebuilt by *Hideyori Toyotomi* and later burnt down in 1787, the only building to survive was the *Shōtenkaku* museum which houses sliding doors and other articles from Kinkakuji Temple. It has an unusual double-roofed *Irimoya* style

43

entrance corridor on the west side. On the ceiling are the works of popular painters of the time such as *Mitsunobu Kanō*. Get off the bus at Dōshisha Daigaku-mae.

● **TADASU-NO-MORI** Tadasu-no-mori is the thickly wooded delta formed by the Kamo and Takano rivers. 'Tadasu' means 'to enquire and get to the bottom of the matter' and it was a traditional place for ordinary people to sort out their disputes. Today, ironically, a family court building stands on the southern edge of the wood.

● **SHIMOGAMO SHRINE** Located close to where the Kamo and Takano rivers meet, this shrine is celebrated for the *Aoi* Festival held annually on May 15. Together with its sister shrine, Kamigamo, it was founded long before

Kyoto became the capital. It was partly rebuilt in 1628, but its main hall dates from 1863. Get off the bus at Shimogamo Jinja-mae.

● **NISHIJIN** This is the district connected with the silk-weaving industry, lying east of Kitano Shrine. The name, meaning 'western camp' dates from the 15th C civil wars.

● **NISHIJIN TEXTILE CENTER** The Center displays a large number of Nishijin products and holds *kimono* shows for group visits. Get off the bus at Horikawa Imadegawa.

● **KITANO TEMMANGU SHRINE** Popularly known as Kitano Tenjin, this shrine was established in 947 to honor *Michizane Sugawara* (845-903), a great scholar, calligrapher and statesman who was deified under the name of Tenjin. After he had been exiled to Kyūshū, his death in 903 was incidentally followed by such severe earthquakes and thunderstorms in Kyoto that it was thought prudent to appease his spirit by erecting a shrine dedicated to him.

The present buildings were constructed in 1607 by *Hideyori Toyotomi*, son of *Hideyoshi Toyotomi* and among the shrine's treasures are a set of nine scrolls illustrating the history of the

Nishijin Textile Center

Kitano Temmangu Shrine

shrine. The grounds contain an extensive grove of trees including hundreds of Japanese apricots, said to have been Michizane's favorite tree. The shrine is now famous for its annual *Baika* (Japanese apricot) festival on Feb 25. Get off the bus at Kitano Temmangū-mae.

SHOPPING & DINING

● *MATSUMAEYA* This is the oldest *Kombu* (sea tangle) shop in Japan, selling beautifully presented kombu produced in Hokkaidō. *Hirome* is particularly recommended.

● *FUKA* Here you can buy fresh *fu* (wheat-gluten bread). Along with *Yuba* (dried bean curd), this is a typical Kyoto delicacy.

● *TAWARAYA YOSHITOMI* A confectionery shop appointed to the Imperial family, one of its more famous delicacies is *Unryū*—a mixture of strained bean jams and rice cake rolled up to represent a dragon riding on a cloud.

● *TSURUYA YOSHINOBU* This store was established in 1803 and one of its well-known products is *Yumochi* — a brownish green, rice based confectionery with a soft delicate taste and citrus aroma.

● *TORAYA KUROKAWA* This noted confectionery store has been appointed to the Imperial family ever since the Nara era and it moved to Kyoto when the capital moved in the Heian era. It is the originator of *neri yōkan* (a sweet jelly made from beans) which it has been making for over 300 years.

● *MANKAMERŌ* This restaurant prepares its cuisine in the traditional Kyoto style with the emphasis on subtle flavors and seasonal ingredients. Its pride is *chakaiseki*, an elegantly presented course of dishes, and they also provide lighter lunches such as *Takekago bentō* (boxed lunch) and accoutrements for afternoon teas. Reservations are necessary.

● *JUTTOKU* This 'Live Spot' is a pioneer in Kyoto's night-life and contains an interesting reconstructed '*sake*' cellar.

45

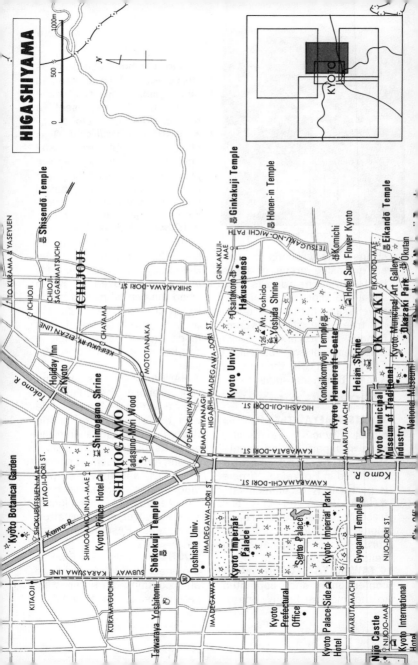

HIGASHIYAMA

KYOTO

0 500 100m

N

Shisendō Temple

ICHIJŌJI

ITO KURAMA & YASEYUEN

Kyōto Botanical Garden

Ginkakuji Temple

Hōnen-in Temple

TETSUGAKU-NO-MICHI PATH

GINKAKUJI-MAE

Osaitōkond

Hakusasonsō

Mt. Yoshida

Yoshida Shrine

126

Komichi

Hotel Sun Flower Kyoto

CHIJŌJI SAGARIMATSUCHO

ICHIJŌJI

SHIRAKAWA-DORI ST.

CHAYAMA

MOTOTANAKA

Kyoto Univ.

Konkaikomyōji Temple

Kyoto Handicraft Center

Heian Shrine

OKAZAKI

Kyoto Municipal Art Gallery

Eikandō Temple

Okutan

Okazaki Park

KEIFUKU RR. EIZAN LINE

Takano R.

Holiday Inn Kyoto

Shimogamo Shrine

DEMACHIYANAGI

DEMACHIYANAGI

HIGASHI-IMADEGAWA-DORI ST.

HIGASHI-OJI-DORI ST.

MARUTA MACHI

Kyoto Municipal Museum of Traditional Industry

Kyoto National Museum

SHIMOGAMO

Tadasuno-Mori Wood

SHOKUBUTSUEN-MAE

KITAOJI-DORI ST.

Kamo R.

SHIMOGAMO-JINJA-MAE

Kyoto Prince Hotel

KARASUMA LINE

SUBWAY

Shōkokuji Temple

KURAMAGUCHI

Doshisha Univ.

IMADEGAWA-DORI ST.

IMADEGAWA

Kyoto Imperial Palace

Kyoto Imperial Park

Sento Palace

Kamo R.

KAWARAMACHI-DORI ST.

KAWABATA-DORI ST.

Kamo R.

KITAOJI

Tawaraya Yoshitomi

Kyoto Prefectural Office

Kyoto Palace-Side Hotel

MARUTAMACHI

Gyoganji Temple

NIJO-DORI ST.

Nijo Castle

NIJOJO-MAE

Kyoto International Hotel

HIGASHIYAMA

This long narrow area, also known as Rakutō, is sand-wiched between the Kamo River flowing north-south through the city and the green Higashiyama hills to the east of the city. Higashiyama, which features countless temples and shrines, is divided into 3 districts. The area around Kiyomizu Temple is a popular walking spot with famous buildings and streets of souvenir stores. Gion is the entertainment area where you may see 'maiko'. The third district lies at the foot of the Higashiyama hills between Nanzenji and Ginkakuji Temples, and is an ideal place for walking.

AROUND KIYOMIZU TEMPLE

With the green Higashiyama hills as a backdrop, this area boasts many temples, shrines and other historical sites. It is a good spot for a stroll and has numerous shops selling traditional crafts and *Kiyomizuyaki* pottery.

WHAT TO SEE

●*SANJŪSANGENDŌ* Sanjūsangendō is the popular name given to the *Rengeōin* Temple, belonging to the *Tendai* sect of Buddhism. It was named for the 33 spaces between the pillars in its elongated structure, some 118m long. Originally erected in 1164, the present hall was rebuilt in 1266 and is well-preserved as a 'National Treasure'. It houses 1,001 wooden Kannon statues, 500 smaller ones on either side of the chief image—the thousand-handed *Senju Kannon*. This masterpiece was carved in 1254 by the celebrated sculptor *Tankei*. Get off the bus at Sanjūsangendō-mae.

The *Hikizome* ceremony, (the first shooting of an arrow in the New Year) originated in

Sanjūsangendō

48

the 16th C, and is performed at the west side of the main hall on Jan 15. Arrows are shot at a target 1m in diameter from a distance of 60m (33 *gen*). Since the arrows appear to fly through the hall, the ceremony is called *Tōshiya* (passing arrows).

● *KYOTO NATIONAL MUSEUM* This museum, north of Sanjū-sangendō, was erected in 1895 by the Imperial Household as a depository for works of art and other treasures belonging to temples, shrines and individuals in Kyoto. The museum has 3 departments: History, Fine Arts and Handicrafts, and its 17 exhibition rooms display over 1,000 art, historical, and religious items. Get off the bus at Higashiyama Shichijō.

● *KYOTO TŌJIKI KAIKAN (KYOTO POTTERY HALL)* This museum displays *Kiyomizu-yaki* pottery and also offers various items for sale, including high quality decorative items at reasonable prices. Get off the bus at Gojōzaka, 2min. walk.

● *HŌKOKU SHRINE* This shrine is formally called Toyokuni Shrine. It is dedicated to *Hideyoshi Toyotomi* whose tomb is here on a mound called *Amidagamine*, east of the main shrine. The original shrine building was magnificent but *Ieyasu Tokugawa* ordered its demolition after the fall of *Toyotomi*. The present buildings, listed as National Treasures, date from 1880. Get off the bus at Sanjūsangendō, 10min. walk.

● *HŌKŌJI TEMPLE* In 1586, a 19m high *Daibutsu* (Great Buddha) was enshrined here. After numerous earthquakes and fires the magnificent temple dedicated to the Great Buddha no longer stands. Of note here is the large bell hanging in the belfry which weighs over 82 tons. It is historically famous for its inscription, reading *Kokka Ankō* (Let the State be at peace), which allegedly provided *Ieyasu Tokugawa* with an excuse to wage war against *Hideyori Toyotomi*. On the north side of Hōkoku Shrine.

● *CHISHAKUIN TEMPLE* This temple was built on the remains of Shōunji Temple by *Hideyoshi Toyotomi* to enshrine his eldest son. Most of its buildings including the *Shoin* and main building date from the Edo era. On the east side of the temple are ornamental ponds and gardens also dating from the early Edo era and storage buildings housing many priceless cul-

49

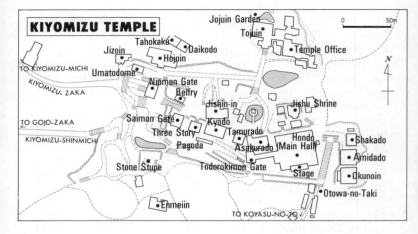

tural works and national treasures. Of special note are Momoyama era paintings such as the famous *Sakura-zu* (The Cherry Tree) and the *Kaede-zu* (The Maple Tree) by *Tōhaku Hasegawa* (a famous 16th C painter) and his adherents. Get off the bus at Higashiyama Shichijō.

● **KAWAI KANJIRO MEMORIAL HALL** This house was built in 1937 by *Kanjirō Kawai* (1890-1966), a world famous potter and proponent of the folkcraft popularization movement in Japan. It contains Kawai's workshop and exhibits of his works. Get off the bus at Umamachi, walk 2min. west.

● *KIYOMIZU TEMPLE* One of Kyoto's most famous temples, Kiyomizu stands on Higashiyama Hill at the top of a narrow road which is called 'Teapot Lane' since it is

crowded with little stores selling *Kiyomizu-yaki* (pottery). Founded in 807, the temple is dedicated to *Jūichi-men*, the 11-headed *Kannon* (Goddess of Mercy) and its present buildings were rebuilt in 1633 by order of *Iemitsu*, the third *Tokugawa Shōgun*.

The main entrance is the 2-story Niōmon Gate, containing in its 2 niches statues of *Kongō-Rikishi*. Get off the bus at Kiyomizu-michi. *Main Hall* Here the 11-headed *Kannon* is enshrined, but perhaps the main attraction is the hall's broad wooden veranda which juts out over a wooded canyon. Supported by 139 pillars, 15m high, it gives a panoramic view of Kyoto. It is the origin of a Japanese proverb, "Jumping from Kiyomizu Veranda" which means to take

Kiyomizu Temple

a determined step.

Saimon (West Gate) Built in 1607, this 8-pillared gate features elaborate carvings and a roof in the orthodox *Kiritsuma* style.

Umatodome Just in front of Niōmon Gate are these stalls where *samurai* would tether their horses when visiting the temple to pray.

Koyasu-no-tō This statue in the 3-storied pagoda south of the main hall, is of the goddess responsible for the safe delivery of babies.Even today it is visited by many pregnant women.

● *SAN-NEN-ZAKA HILL & NINEN-ZAKA HILL* Sannen-zaka consists of stone steps linking Kiyomizu-zaka and Ninen-zaka (Two-year Hill). Most of the shops lining the sides of the hill are wooden houses from the Edo era selling *Kiyomizu-yaki*, special Kyoto food and traditional souvenirs. Ninen-zaka is the street leading from Sannen-zaka (Three-year Hill) to Kōdaiji. Get off the bus at Kiyomizu-dō.

● *ROKUHARAMITSUJI TEMPLE* This temple was founded in 963 by *Kūya Shōnin*, an eminent priest. He carved an image of the 11-headed *Kannon* (Goddess of Mercy) and installed it in the temple in the hope of stopping a pestilence raging in Kyoto at the time. The temple was destroyed many times but still

51

KIYOMIZU-YAKI

Kyō-yaki is the name given to the pottery and ceramics produced in Kyoto and its representative style is *Kiyomizu-yaki*, produced in the area around Kiyomizu Temple. Pottery began in Kyoto in the 8th C and by the 17th C had developed into ten different schools, but now only the *Kiyomizu-yaki* style remains. It consists mainly of porcelain and is divided into the types known as *Seiji* (blue-painted), *Aka-e*(red-painted) and *Some-tsuke* (enameled).

contains many Buddhist works of art and sculptures, including images of the Maharajas (Four Heavenly Guardians) by *Unkei* and a statue of *Taira-no-Kiyomori*, the head of the *Taira* clan. Get off the bus at Kiyomizu-michi, walk 5min.

SHOPPING & DINING

● **OKAMOTO-ORIMONO-TEN** This specialty store sells Japanese fabrics and *kimono*s including *Nishijin* brocade and the famous *Tatsumura* products. For souvenirs, there are numerous bags, purses and pouches.

●*EBIYA RYŪZAN* A traditional *Kiyomizu-yaki* pottery shop dating from 1782. It contains a kiln and produces a variety of reasonably priced pottery for sale.

●*FŪGADŌ* This store, marked by an enormous lantern at the entrance, sells traditional bone-framed products including old trays, *sake* containers, large drums, oil paper umbrellas, Buddhist figurines, combs and ornamental hairpins.

● **SHICHIMIYA** Wafting through this old store is the smell of *Shichimi tōgarashi*—a blend of 7 kinds of cayenne pepper. They also sell attractive bamboo or pottery pepper containers.

●**WARAJIYA** The large sign hanging outside this establishment indicates it is an eel restaurant. It is famous for its *u-zōsui*—eel rice gruel with a light taste. Reservations needed for 3 or more people.

●**KASAGIYA** The main delicacies of this *Oshirukoya* (traditional tea shop) are its *Oshiruko* and *Ohagi* sweet dishes. It has a cozy atmosphere and is particularly popular with young ladies.

GION & MARUYAMA

This tea shop district abounds in old temples, shops and restaurants. Its unhurried atmosphere and the chance to see traditional sights such as *Maiko* strolling around attract people here. *Miyako-odori* (Kyoto Dancing) is also performed here in different ceremonies such as the Gion Fes-

Shichimiya

tival.

WHAT TO SEE

●*KEN-NINJI TEMPLE* This temple is the origin of the *Rinzai* sect of Buddhism in Japan, as well as the headquarters of its *Kenninji* school. It was founded in 1202 by priest *Eisai* after returning from his second visit to China, then under the Sung Dynasty. The original buildings were destroyed by fire with the exception of the Chokushimon Gate. The superior's apartments were reputedly built by the first *Ashikaga* shōgun *Takauji* (1305-1358), at Ankokuji Temple in Aki Province (now Hiroshima Prefecture) and later moved to this site. The temple houses several scroll paintings by *Yūshō Kaihō* and is famous for a painted screen now exhibited in the Kyoto National Museum. The screen depicts 'Demons creating Wind and Thunder' by *Sōtatsu Tawaraya,* who flourished in the early 17th C.

Ryōsoku-in This is a small temple in the grounds of Kenninji Temple, well-known for the paintings on its sliding screens, attributed to *Tōhaku Hasegawa*, and for the beauty of the garden with its springs and ponds. Get off the bus at Higashiyama-yasui, walk 3min. west.

●*MINAMIZA THEATER* This is the nation's oldest theater, one of the few remaining from the Edo era. It features all-star cast *Kabuki* performances and is known for its December ceremony where new actors announce the start of their careers. Get off the bus at Shijō Keihan-mae.

● *GION* This is the best known of the traditional *geisha* quarters in Kyoto and best preserves the atmosphere of olden times. Originally it was an area for people to relax and be served tea after visiting Yasaka Shrine. The area gradually changed and by the middle of the 18th C it had become known as the largest entertainment area in Kyoto. Kimono-clad *maiko* and *geigi* (*geisha*) can often be seen here. Get off the bus at Gion.

●*GION CORNER* Situated on the 11th floor of Yasaka Kaikan Hall in Gion, this offers visitors a chance to enjoy traditional Japanese arts. Twice daily there are demonstrations of tea ceremony and flower arrangement, as well as performances of *Bunraku* (puppets), *Kyōgen* (comic interludes), *Kyō-mai* (Kyoto-style dance), *Koto* music and *Gagaku* (ancient court music

53

with dancing). Get off the bus at Higashiyama-yasui or Gion.

● **KYOTO HANDICRAFT CENTER** The Center displays and sells traditional Japanese handicraft items. As well as goods produced in Kyoto, there are handicrafts from all over Japan including laquerware, fans, silk products, *kimonos* and pearl and coral accessories. There is also a coffee shop and a gallery. Get off the bus at Kumano Jinja-mae.

● **MARUYAMA PARK** This is the principal public park in Kyoto and includes an extremely beautiful landscape garden laid out at the foot of Higashiyama, just east of Yasaka Shrine. The center of the park contains hundreds of cherry trees. When in blossom, they are illuminated at night and attract crowds of people. Get off the bus at Gion and walk 2min. east.

● **YASAKA SHRINE** The shrine is situated at the eastern end

Yasaka Shrine

of Gion Machi and is commonly called "Gion-san". It is dedicated to the Shintō deities *Susano-o-no-Mikoto* and his consort *Inadahime-no-Mikoto*, together with their sons.

The present buildings, with the exception of the older 2-story west gate, were built in 1654 by order of the shōgun. The granite *torii* on the south side, erected in 1666, stands 9.5m high and is one of the largest in Japan. The main shrine is a single-story building with a roof covered with *Keyaki* wood shingles and constructed in what is called the *Gion* style. Among the shrine's treasures are a pair

GION FESTIVAL

Starting on July 1 and continuing for a month, this huge festival took its present form in the Edo era, when the sumptuously decorated floats first made their appearance. The main events are the *Yoi-yama*, on the 16th, and the *Yamahoko-junkō*, on the 17th, when the floats are paraded to the accompaniment of flutes, drums and gongs.

of carved wooden *Komainu*—mythological animals attributed to the renowned sculptor *Unkei*. The shrine is the site of the *Gion* Festival and *Okera Mairi* — two of Kyoto's most noteworthy festivals. Get off the bus at Gion.

● *CHION-IN TEMPLE* The temple is set in large grounds at the north end of Maruyama Park and is the headquarters of the *Jōdo* sect. It was built in 1234 by Priest *Genchi*, a disciple of *Hōnen*, the founder of this *Zen* sect. The present buildings were mostly built in the Edo era with the assistance of the *Tokugawa* shogunate, and the temple was considerably expanded to become one of the largest and best-known in Japan.

The temple houses many works of art, including 48 volumes of an illustrated biography of *Hōnen*, registered as a National Treasure, reputedly painted by *Yoshimitsu Tosa* in the early 14th C. Get off the bus at Chion-in-mae, walk 5min. east.

Sammon (Front Gate) This 2-story structure, 24m high, was built in 1619 and is considered the most imposing of all temple gates in Japan.

Hondō (Main Hall) Built by the third *Tokugawa* shōgun in 1639, the hall is dedicated to *Hōnen* and his statue, which he carved, is housed in a laquered shrine in the innermost part of the hall. The corridor behind the main hall, leading to the assembly hall, was built by master carpenter *Jingorō Hidari*. At every step the floorboards emit sounds resembling the *Uguisu* (Japanese bush warbler).

Daihōjō, Shōhōjō (Superior's Apartments) The sliding screens in these apartments are decorated with beautiful paintings in the *Kanō* style by *Naonobu* and *Nobumasa* in the 17th C.

Daishōrō On the southeast side of the temple stands the famous belfry with its huge bell, the largest of its kind in Japan. It is 2.7m in diameter and weighs 74 tons.

● *SHOREN-IN TEMPLE* Located north of Chion-in, this temple is popularly called Awata Palace, from the name of the road it faces. It is well-known as the former residence of

55

Chion-in Temple

Shōren-in Temple

head abbots of the *Tendai* sect. It was founded in 1150,

but the present buildings date from 1895. The garden, designed partly by *Sōami* and partly by *Enshū*, is regarded as one of the finest landscape gardens in Kyoto. Get off the bus at Jingūmichi, walk 5min.

WHAT TO BUY

● **HIGASHIYAMA KOGEI** This shop exudes all the old-world atmosphere of Kyoto and sells unusual handicrafts and sundries. Interesting items include goods made from cloth *sake* containers such as

GION & MARUYAMA

N 200m

Sanjo-Ohashi Bridge

KEIHAN RY. KYOZU LINE

HIGASHIYAMA-SANJO

SANJO-DORI ST.

SANJO

Nakamura-Chingireten

Shōren-in Temple

Shirakawa R.

HIGASHI-OJI-DORI ST.

HANAMI-KOJI-DORI ST.

NAWATE-DORI ST.

PONTOCHO-DORI ST.

KEIHAN RY. MAIN LINE

Kamo R.

CHION-IN-MAE

Chion-in Temple

Choboya

Gion Kaikan

Hiranoya Honten

Oranda Kagizen-Yoshifusa

Kyoto Craft Center

Shijo-Ohashi Bridge

SHIJO-DORI ST.

GION

Maruyama Park

SHIJO

Minamiza Theater

Kawabun

Yamafuku

Yasaka Shrine

Chorakukan

Chorakuji Temple

Ippei Jaya

GION

Minoko

Otani Hombyo Temple

TO GOJO

Yasaka-Kaikan Bldg. (1F. Gion Corner)

Higashiyama-Kōgei

Ken-ninji Temple

Gion Kobukaburenjo Theater

HIGASHIYAMA-YASUI

Bun-no-suke Jaya

Kodaiji Temple

Ryozen Kannon Temple

Miyagawacho Kaburenjo Theater

TO KIYOMIZUMICHI

TO NINEN-ZAKA

56

wallets and wall hangings. They have printed patterns and come in attractive dark-brown colors, the result of a natural dyeing process.

● *KAWABUN* Originally this store sold art items but now is better known for its stock of Japanese dyed paper and other paper goods. These handmade, hand-dyed goods include dolls, miniature chests of drawers and dressing tables — all made from *chiyogami* paper. As well as paper products, the exquisite, high-quality paper itself can be bought.

●*NAKAMURA CHINGIRE* *Chingire*, also known as *kodaigire*, are old, woven and dyed fabrics printed in a variety of patterns. The store also stocks different brocades and *yūzen* and indigo dyed goods.

● *CHOBOYA* This footwear store sells *okobo*, the shoes worn by maiko as well as *zōri* and *geta*. It also stocks *tabi* (socks), umbrellas and decorative miniature *geta* and black-laquered shoes.

WHERE TO EAT

● *BUN-NO-SUKE JAYA* This tea shop serves *Amazake*—a sweet drink made from fermented rice and usually mixed with grated ginger. Other combinations include *warabi-mochi*, rice-flour dumplings.

●*MINOKŌ* A fascinating restaurant where you can appreciate the true flavor and artful presentation of Kyoto *Chakaiseki* (pre-tea ceremony) cuisine. A reasonably-priced *bentō* (boxed lunch) is also served.

● *CHORAKUKAN* This shop has all the appearance of a museum but is actually a coffee shop. It is in a Meiji era, western-style building that was formerly a guest house.

●*ORANDA* This is a cozy French restaurant decorated with Japanese paintings and varieties of fans. Its shrimp gratin and *Oranda-Yaki* (Dutch steaks) are popular.

●*IPPEI JAYA* This old traditional shop sells the perfect accompaniment to Kyoto's winter: *Kaburamushi* (steamed turnip). The dish includes turnips from *Shōgoin*

57

Minokō

Hiranoya

temple, sea bream, eel and seasonal vegetables.

● **HIRANOYA** Boasting a 300 year history, this shop is most famous for its *Imobō* — a mixture of dried cod and potato.

● **KAGIZEN YOSHIFUSA** This 200 year old store is famous for its *Kuzukiri* (chopped arrowroot) from which is made arrowroot starch (agar jelly) like transparent noodles.

NIGHTLIFE

● **MAHARAJAH** Even *maiko* are sometimes seen at this extremely popular and lively disco. The Buddhist statues decorating the dance floor contribute to its 'oriental' atmosphere and it serves a wide selection of food and drink.

● **MOUSTACHE** A chic café bar tastefully decorated in navy blue and gray. The background music — Jazz and the Bossa nova — plays at just the right level.

● **YAMAFUKU** With its lattice-work facade, and serene, traditional style interior, this friendly bar perfectly suits its Gion district setting. It features a menu of simple home-cooked dishes.

NANZENJI TEMPLE AREA

This is the area skirting the foot of the Higashiyama mountains from Nanzenji Temple to Ginkakuji Temple. The Heian Shrine and Kyoto University are here and the foothills are dotted with temples and shrines, giving the area a mood of tranquility. In former times, the aristocracy were attracted by this peaceful, quiet place and built their retreats here. Due to those beginnings, today it is an area of expensive housing. It was the birthplace of Higashiyama culture and today is an excellent place to escape to for a peaceful stroll around its shrines and temples.

WHAT TO SEE

● **NANZENJI TEMPLE** Situated in a pine grove east of the Heian Shrine, this temple is the headquarters of the *Nan-*

zenji school of the *Rinzai* sect. It is the foremost of the sect's five great Kyoto temples and is a beautiful example of 13th—17th C art and craft. Originally, it was a detached palace belonging to Emperor *Kameyama* (1249-1305) and was given to a priest and converted into a temple in 1291. The buildings have repeatedly been destroyed by fire and rebuilt, however some of the 17th C structures remain.

Sammon The main entrance to the temple, this huge wooden gate was built in 1628. The ceiling is decorated with paintings of angels and birds, attributed to artists of the *Tosa* and *Kanō* schools.

Hōjō (Superior's Quarters) This National Treasure consists of 2 buildings, the larger one was the former *Seiryōden* of the Imperial Palace, donated to the temple in 1611. The splendid paintings on its sliding screens were done by artists of the *Kanō* school. The smaller suite formerly formed part of *Hideyoshi*'s Fushimi castle, and features famous murals of 'Tigers in a Bamboo Grove' by *Tan-yū Kanō*.

Hōjō Garden This is a typical example of the *Karesansui* style with white sand re-

presenting the ocean and rocks and plants representing an earthly paradise or Shangri-la. Get off the bus at Keage or Eikandō-mae, walk 10min.

● **TETSUGAKU-NO-MICHI (PATH OF PHILOSOPHY)** This pleasant walking path runs alongside the canal from Nyakuōji Bridge to Ginkakuji Temple Bridge, a distance of about 2km. The path is so named because *Kitarō Nishida*, a philosopher, used to walk along here, lost in thought. There are numerous small bridges spanning the canal, and the path has many benches where strollers can sit and admire the cherry, laurel and chestnut trees in different seasons.

● **EIKANDŌ** Eikandō is the popular name for *Zenrinji* Temple and is well-known for its unrivaled autumn scenery.

59

Tetsugaku-no-Michi

Ginkakuji Temple

The main building houses a famous statue of Amitabha Buddha, in a pose looking back over his shoulder. Also of note is the corridor called *Garyūrō*, with its many bends and turns, which was built entirely without nails. Get off the bus at Eikandō-mae, walk 10min. east.

● **GINKAKUJI TEMPLE (SILVER-PAVILION)** This is the popular name of *Jishōji* Temple belonging to the *Shōkokuji* school of the *Rinzai* sect. One of Kyoto's most beautiful sights, it was originally built in 1482 as a country villa by *Yoshimasa Ashikaga*, the military ruler in the 15th C. He intended to have the pavilion covered with silver leaf, but due to his sudden death the plan never saw fruition. Hence it remains 'Silver Pavilion' in

name only. On his death the villa was converted into a temple.

The main hall contains an image of Buddha, while the **Tōgudō** houses an effigy of *Yoshimasa Ashikaga* in the garb of a priest. In the northeast corner of the same building is a tiny tearoom, said to be the oldest in Japan. (Closed to the public).

Ginkakuji Garden was laid out in 1482 by *Sōami*, a painter and garden designer. It is famous for its exquisite beauty and design and contains a white sand cone, *Kōgetsudai*, designed to reflect moonlight and enhance the beauty of the garden at night. Get off the bus at Ginkakuji-mae, walk 5min.

● **HAKUSASONSO** In the grounds of Ginkakuji Temple is the house where the painter *Kansetsu Hashimoto* lived. Built in 1916, the house contains his eclectic art collection, including works from China, Greece, India and Per-

Hakusasonso's Stone Statue

sia. The garden here is a very pretty pond-centered strolling garden and is known for the "borrowed scenery" provided by the mountain rising in the background. Near Ginkakuji-mae bus stop.

● **KYOTO UNIVERSITY** Founded in 1869, this is the largest state university after the University of Tokyo and has an enrolment of over 15,000. The university has faculties of Education, Literature, Agriculture, Science, Engineering, Medecine and Pharmaceutical Science and a hospital. Get off the bus at Hyakumamben.

● **OKAZAKI PARK** The park covers an area of 8.5 ha. along the canal leading from Lake Biwa. It was opened to the public in 1904 and contains the Kyoto Prefectural Central Library, the Public Hall, the Kyoto Municipal Art Gallery, the Municipal Zoological Garden and a sports stadium.

The public library is the oldest in Japan, having been established in 1872. On its premises is a monument to Gottfried Wagner, a German who was invited to Kyoto in 1878 to make improvements in the traditional dyeing and ceramic arts of Kyoto. The zoo gardens have a large number of cherry and maple

Murin-an Villa

trees, making an attractive scene in spring and winter. Near Okazaki kōen-mae bus stop.

● **MURIN-AN VILLA** Located near Kyoto Zoological Garden and Nanzenji Temple, this villa was built in the Meiji era by the well-known statesman, *Aritomo Yamagata* (1838-1922). The grounds contain the wooden main building, a Japanese-style tearoom and a Western-style annex that is a good example of typical Meiji era architecture. The villa's serene garden has small streams flowing through it and is another pond-centered 'borrowed scenery' garden, making use of Mt. Higashiyama in the background. 5 min. walk from Dōbutsukōen-mae bus stop.

● **HEIAN SHRINE** One of Kyoto's newer shrines, it was built in 1895 to mark the

61

1,100th anniversary of the founding of Kyoto by Emperor *Kammu* (737 — 806). The shrine structures, with the exception of the concrete *torii* are reconstructions on a 5/8 scale of buildings that stood in the Imperial Court of the Heian era, and it gives us some of the flavor of that era and the old capital.

The shrine consists of the East and West **Honden** (Main Halls), the two towers *Byakko* (White Tiger) and *Sōryū* (Blue Dragon) and the **Ōtemmon** (Main Gate). The 2-storied Ōtemmon Gate is a replica of

JIDAI MATSURI (FESTIVAL OF THE AGES)

One of Kyoto's largest festivals, this grand spectacle began in 1895, on the 1,100th anniversary of the transference of the capital to Kyoto. Held every year on October 22, the festival features a huge spectacular parade, with over 2,000 costumed marchers in 17 groups. The procession depicts Japan's history and culture from the Meiji era back through the ages to the Heian era. The parade leaves the Kyoto Imperial Palace at noon and takes about two and a half hours to reach the Heian shrine.

The procession starts with the Meiji era (1868-1912) and a parade recalling the *Ishin Kinno-tai*, the Imperial army at the time of the Meiji Restoration. Following is the Edo era (1603-1868), with a parade of women wearing *uchikake*, a coat worn over kimono on ceremonial occasions. The parade representing the Azuchi-Momoyama era (1573-1603) depicts the warrior general *Toyotomi Hideyoshi* in full armor, with his retinue proceeding to pay their respects to the Emperor. Part of this procession features an elaborately decorated ox-drawn carriage.

The Kamakura era (1192-1333) is represented by a *Yabusame* (archers on horseback) parade, common among the samurai. In the Heian era (794-1192) parade, spectators are delighted by the sight of a procession of ladies, including *Onono Komachi*, a poetess of the early Heian era who is said to have been a woman of peerless beauty.

Jidai Matsuri

SHOPPING & DINING

Along the approach to Nan-zenji Temple and through the Chokushimon, there are a lot of restaurants devoted to *Yudōfu* (boiled *tōfu*: bean curd), a specialty of the Nan-zenji area. Two of the best known of these are Junsei and Okutan. Osaitokoro, in the corner of *Hakusasonso*.

the main gate of the Imperial Court. The shrine has a very beautiful garden, well-known for its wisteria, weeping cherries and irises. The *Jidai Matsuri* held here on Oct 22 is one of Kyoto's most spectacular fetes. Get off the bus at Kyoto Kaikan Bijutsukan-mae and walk 2min. north.

When walking along the Tetsugaku-no-michi, **Komi-chi**, is a good tea-room to stop off at. In the Okazaki area can be found the famous **Hyōtei**, which serves *Cha-kaiseki* (pre-tea ceremony cuisine). The setting, decor and food all help make this a respected establishment. Recommended is the summer rice gruel '*Asagayu*'. For take-home samples of Kyoto's renowned confectionery, the very best is probably *Yatsuha-shi*, which is *sembei* (rice cracker) flavored with cinnamon.

●**KYOTO MUNICIPAL MUSEUM OF TRADITIONAL INDUSTRY** The center offers visitors a good one-stop look at a variety of traditional Kyoto arts and crafts. Exhibits and demonstrations here include *yūzen* dyed fabrics, embroidery, *Kiyomizu-yaki* and *Awata-yaki* porcelain, laquer-ware, Kyoto dolls, *shippō* (cloisonne), *sensu* (folding fans), and damascene work as well as a variety of bamboo, silk, and paper products and handicrafts. Get off the bus at Kyoto Kaikan Bijutsukan-mae.

63

Yudōfu Cooking

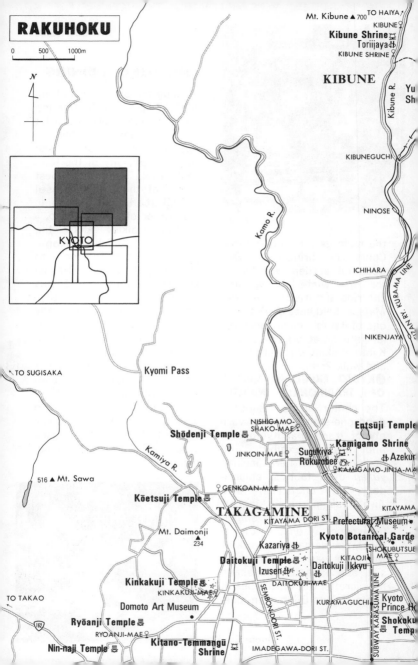

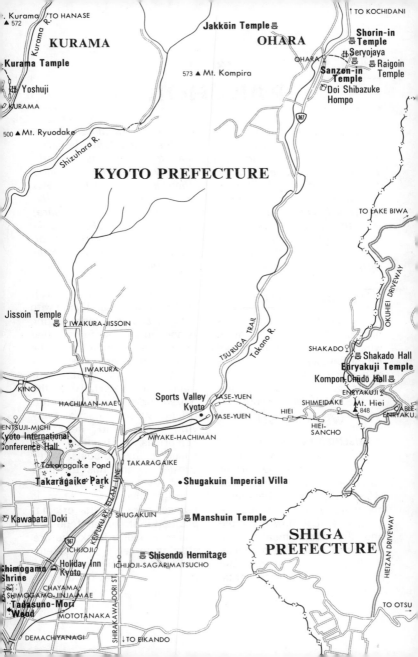

RAKUHOKU

Rakuhoku, also called Kitayama (Northern Mountains), lies to the north of central Kyoto. Its steep mountains, believed since ancient times to be the haunts of evil spirits, still retain an atmosphere of mystery today. Rakuhoku is divided into four areas: the eastern urban areas of Ichijōji and Shūgakuin; Kamigamo and Murasakino in the center; the outlying Rakuhoku area including Kurama, Kibune and Ōhara; and the mountainous area from Mt. Hiei to Lake Biwa in Shiga Prefecture. Although Rakuhoku's numerous places of interest are scattered over a large area, bus and train networks make the area easily accessible.

ICHIJOJI & SHUGAKUIN

Shirakawa Street runs northsouth through this area, which is situated above Kitashirakawa. Here, farms and rice paddies can still be found, giving glimpses of life on the outskirts of Kyoto.

WHAT TO SEE

● **SHISENDŌ Hermitage** This hermitage was built in 1641 as the retreat of the former *samurai jōzan Ishikawa* (1583-1672), who abandoned his military life and became a recluse. It is now a temple and the name means 'Hall of the Great Poets' since it displays the poems and portraits of 36 Chinese poets. It is also known for its Chinese garden which features white sand lined with pruned azaleas, representing islands in the sea. Surrounded by maples, it imparts a calm beauty in every season. A stream flows from the man-made waterfall to the *Shishi-odoshi*, a device originally used to scare away wild boar and deer. It comprises a bamboo pipe supported by two posts. Water trickles in and fills the pipe which then swings down and releases the water. When it swings back to its original position it strikes a stone and makes a hollow 'tonk', before starting to refill. This serene sound has fascinated people for centuries. Get off the bus at Ichijoji Sagari-Matsuchō, walk 10 min. southeast.

● *MANSHUIN TEMPLE*

Manshuin Temple, surrounded by groves of maples and cryptomerias, somewhat resembles Katsura Imperial Villa in its stately, graceful appearance. The temple buildings were moved to and for several times before finally being constructed on this site in 1656. The temple is known for the care given to details in its design, including its interesting openwork railings.

The temple's garden is a typical *Karesansui* rock garden with rocks representing the flow of a waterfall, stone bridges, and islands of rocks representing cranes and turtles laid out in a sea of gravel. 30min. walk northeast of Shisendō.

● *SHŪGAKUIN IMPERIAL VILLA*

This villa is located at the foot of Mt. Hiei, on the former site of the Heian era temple, *Shūgakuin*. It was originally built by the *Tokugawa* Shogunate as a retreat for ex-Emperor *Gomizuno-o*. The villa consists of 3 summer houses, each built in a large garden on a different level, along with a temple, tea-ceremony houses and other buildings within a total area of 28ha.

The gardens are the largest and most elegant of Kyoto's numerous pond-centered, strolling gardens. The upper garden (*Kamino Chaya*) and lower garden (*Shimono Chaya*) were laid out in 1659, and the middle one (*Nakano Chaya*) was completed in 1682. In 1884, control of the villa was transferred to the Imperial Household Agency.

For visits to the villa, advance permission in person is required from the Kyoto office of the Imperial Household Agency, located in the Kyoto Imperial Palace. Get off the bus at Shūgakuin-rikyūmichi, walk 10 min. east.

KAMIGAMO & MURASAKINO

This area, the northern extremity of Kyoto city,

Manshuin Temple

67

ranges from Takaragaike Pond in the east to Takagamine in the west. It features many old temples and shrines, including the well-known Daitokuji Temple.

WHAT TO SEE

● **TAKARAGAIKE PARK** This lovely park, with its many promenades, is set among beautiful stands of trees and features Takaragaike pond at its center. To the east of the ponds stands the Kyoto International Conference Hall, which was built in the traditional *Gasshō zukuri* style of architecture. It is open to the public and includes a restaurant and coffee shop. Get off the bus at Takaragaike kōen-mae.

● **ENTSŪJI TEMPLE** This temple was originally built as a residence for ex-Emperor *Gomizuno-o* but was later used as a convent. It is well-known for its "borrowed scenery" garden which makes use of Mt. Hiei as a spectacular backdrop. The *Karesansui* style rock and sand garden features about 40 artfully arranged moss-covered rocks and is bordered with a hedge of azalea and 'sasanqua' trees. Get off the bus at Entsūjimichi and walk 10 min. west.

● **KAMO RIVER** Starting at Mt. Sajikigatake, this river flows southwards to meet the Katsura River. It often flooded in the Heian era but the volume of water has since decreased. With its banks lined with willow and cherry trees, the river is a pleasant place for a stroll.

● **KYOTO BOTANICAL GARDEN** Opened in 1924, this garden occupies a 240,000sq.m site and its beautiful gardens are an attraction at any time of the year. They include a western-style garden, a rose garden, cherry garden, herb garden and rows of camphor trees. It also contains a very large tropical greenhouse, a library and a Memorial Hall. Get off the bus at Kyoto Shokubutsuen-mae.

● **KAMIGAMO SHRINE** Kamigamo Shrine and Shimogamo Shrine are actually the upper and lower

Kamigamo Shrine

halves of the same shrine, both dedicated to *Raijin*, the god of thunder. One of Kyoto's oldest shrines, Shimogamo reputedly dates from the 7th C, before the Heian era. The present buildings date from the 17th to 19th centuries but as faithful representations of the ancient style, they are extremely interesting. The shrine is famous for the *Aoi* Festival in May and a holy horse race, *Kurabe-uma*, an event held to protect the rice harvest. Get off the bus at Kamigamojinja-mae.

● *SHŌDENJI TEMPLE* The temple is approached by climbing a long flight of old stone steps, through a thick grove of trees. Shōdenji was established in the Kamakura era and the original buildings, with the exception of the main hall and warehouse, were destroyed by fire. A feature of the temple are the wooden boards of the *Chi-Tenjō*, (Blood Ceiling). These were once used as flooring on the corridor where 1,200 people committed suicide after hearing of the surrender of Fushimi Castle. Get off the bus at Shinkōin-mae, walk 15 min. northeast.

● *DAITOKUJI TEMPLE* One of Kyoto's most important temples, Daitokuji was

69

founded in 1315 and is the headquarters of the *Rinzai* sect. It was frequently burnt down during the period of civil war and the present buildings are mostly reconstructions dating from the 16th C. The grounds contain over 20 *Tatchū*, (minor temple buildings), which were built in memory of various deceased military commanders. The temple also contains the tomb of *Sen-no-Rikyū*, a tea master of the Momoyama era who established a new, highly artistic style of tea ceremony called 'wabicha'. Thus, Daitokuji is considered holy ground by all the *Sadō* (Tea Ceremony) schools and there are many tea-ceremony rooms here.

The **Sammon** (Main Gate) was erected in 1589 by *Sen-no-Rikyū*. Its lower story features dragons and other decorations, the work of *Tōhaku Hasegawa* (1539-1610).

The **Butsuden** (Main Hall) dates from 1664 while the **Hattō** (Lecture Hall) was rebuilt in 1636 at the rear of the Butsuden. The **Hōjō** (Superior's Residence) features sliding screens decorated with paintings by *Tan-yū Kanō*.

Daisen-in This temple and other subsidiary temples of Daitokuji have elegant gardens, laid out in the early 17th C. **Hōjō garden** in Daisen-in is a masterpiece of the *Karesansui* dry landscape style and ranks with the famous rock garden in Ryōanji Temple. Skilful use is made of trees, rocks and sand to express the majesty of nature, from waterfalls to valleys and lakes.

Zuihōin This is a family temple enshrining the feudal lord, *Sōrin Ōtomo*, who was a Christian. The stones in its rock garden are arranged in the shape of a crucifix. Get off the bus at Daitokuji-mae.

● **KŌETSUJI TEMPLE** Built in 1615, this temple was formerly the hermitage of *Kōetsu Hon-ami*, a renowned gold-laquer artist of the Edo era. After his death it was reconstructed as a temple, dedicated to the repose of his soul. As well as the Main Hall and Warehouse, the grounds contain five tea-ceremony houses. In the temple grounds is a well-known fence called '*Kōetsu-gaki*', made with slats of interwoven bamboo. Get off the bus at Genkōan-mae, walk 3min. west.

● **KITAYAMA STREET** Ginkgo trees line this popular street which attracts young and fashion-conscious shoppers with its many modish boutiques and stylish restaurants. It is a pleasant place to windowshop and the banks of the Kamo River, running to the west of the street, are ideal for a quiet, leisurely stroll. Get off the bus at Kitayamabashi

Higashizume.

SHOPPING & DINING

● *DAITOKUJI IKKYU* This historic establishment has been serving vegetarian cuisine for over 500 years. It is famous for its *Daitokuji Nattō* sauce, originally prepared by the priest *Ikkyū*. Careful preparation characterizes all of its dishes.

● *IZUSEN* Located near Daitokuji Temple, this restaurant serves vegetarian dishes in vermillion-lacquered, tin bowls. This preserves an old custom since these kind of bowls were used by Buddhist priests for eating, washing and religious practices.

● *CAPITAL TOYOTEI HONTEN* This western-style restaurant has a light, bright atmosphere and a lawn with white tables and chairs. Recommended are their seafood dishes. Coffee is also available in the restaurant's sunroom.

● *KAZARIYA* Located near the east exit of Imamiya Shrine, this shop serves ricecakes. They are coated with soybean flour and grilled over a charcoal fire and served with a sweet bean paste.

● *SUGUKIYA ROKUROBEE* Here you can try *Suguki zuke*, pickles of the radishes

Daitokuji Ikkyu

harvested in Kyoto. They are prepared in the traditional style using no artificial preservatives.

● *AZEKURA* This is a noodle shop, built in rustic style with large pine and cypress beams and featuring earth floors. Thick, hand-made noodles are their specialty.

● *GARACIA* This specialty glass shop sells work by young Kyoto craftsmen as well as pieces from around Japan and imports from the U.S.A. and Mexico.

● *KAWABATADOKI* This store sells *Chimaki*, steamed rice dumplings wrapped in bamboo leaves. Specialties are *Yōkan chimaki* and *Suisen chimaki* both filled with sweet bean jelly.

OUTSKIRTS OF RAKUHOKU

This section introduces places of interest away from the city area, such as the

71

quiet shrines and temples at the foot of Mt. Kurama and Mt. Kibune and the temples in Ōhara. Hikers may consider the short hiking course near Kurama. Getting there is not a problem. The Eizan Railway and buses take you to Kurama and in Ōhara, transport is available for visitors to the temples.

WHAT TO SEE

● *KURAMA TEMPLE* Mt. Kurama has been feared since ancient times as a haunt of evil spirits and robbers. Kurama Temple, which stands on the side of the mountain, is famous as the place where *Minamoto-no-Yoshitsune* a military commander of the powerful *Genji* family is said to have undergone spiritual training with one of the long-nosed and winged goblins known as *Tengu*. On October 22, the *Kurama-no-Himatsuri*, one of Japan's three biggest 'curious festivals' is held here. In this fire festival, young men wearing loincloths parade around waving huge 5m-high pine torches.

From Kurama Temple, there is a 1.2km. (50min.) hiking course through forest to Kibune Shrine. The course starts from the temple's main hall. Get off the bus at Kurama. From the temple gate, 30 min. walk to the main hall.

● *KIBUNE SHRINE* This old shrine was erected long before the Heian capital was established in 794. It was built as a place to worship the god of water, long revered by brewers and farmers. When you leave the very quiet,

---

DAIMONJI GOZAN OKURIBI

Held on Aug. 16, this festival is one of the many ceremonies of *Bon*, the time when the souls of ancestors are thought to return to this world. In the festival, fires called *okuribi* are lit to speed the souls on their way back after their yearly visit. Fires are lit on five hills (*Gozan*) around Kyoto, in the shape of the Chinese characters *dai* (large), *myō* (miraculous) and *ho* (doctrine) and in the shape of a *Funagata* (ship) and *torii* (shrine gate).

Sanzen-in Temple

entitled *Bosatsu Raigō*. This depicts Bodhisattvas descending from heaven to save mankind.

The temple has two gardens, *Yūsei-en* and *Shuheki-en*, both of which are surrounded by cryptomeria and maple trees and contain ponds and fountains. Get off the bus at Ōhara, walk 10min. west.

● *SHŌRIN-IN TEMPLE* This temple is well-known as the place where the founder of the *Jōdo* sect, *Hōnen Shōnin*, exchanged religious views with the rural magistrate. The grounds contain the main hall and a small belfry. Jikkōin and Hōsen-in, branches of Shōrin-in, are located nearby. 2 min. walk north of Sanzen-in Temple.

● *JAKKOIN TEMPLE* Located west of Sanzen-in Temple, Jakkōin temple is a convent built on a perfectly secluded site. It is famous as the place where the Empress *Kenreimon-in*, mother of the infant Emperor *Antoku*, became a nun in 1185. She spent the rest of her life here after her imperial son perished along with the rest of the *Taira* clan at *Dan-no-ura* (the present Shimonoseki, in western Japan). Her tomb lies on a hill

peaceful shrine grounds, there is a lively little street dotted with restaurants serving river-fish dishes. Get off the bus at Kibune-jinja-mae (one bus daily). Or from Kibune-guchi stop, walk 30 min. north. (four buses daily)

● *SANZEN-IN TEMPLE*
Sanzen-in Temple was built at Ōhara as a residence for the brothers and sisters of deified emperors. The site was chosen since Ōhara had been considered a holy place from ancient times by believers in *Jōdo*, the Pure Land or Buddhist Heaven. The temple consists of a beautiful mansion and gardens set in secluded hills.

The main hall, *Ōjō Gokuraku-in*, is said to have been built in 1148 and is dedicated to Amitabha. It has a beautifully symmetric design, with the eaves sweeping upwards. Its unusual ceiling is shaped like the bottom of a boat and is decorated with the painting

73

behind the temple. The convent's garden is regarded as one of the finest places for maple-viewing in Kyoto. Get off the bus at Ōhara, walk 20 min. west.

SHOPPING & DINING

Yōshūji was the original name of Kurama Road, where you can find a restaurant called Yōshūji. Here you can enjoy seasonal dishes and a decor that reproduces the interior of old Japanese farmhouses. Toriijaya is a restaurant near the great 'torii' gate of Kibune Shrine. Recommended is its *Chamise bentō*, a box-lunch containing assorted wild vegetables and portions of river-fish. On the path up the slope to Sanzen-in Temple in Ōhara stand numerous tea shops and restaurants. One of these, Seryōjaya, boasts a specialty of buckwheat noodles topped with grated yam. Another dish, which will satisfy your curiosity about wild vegetables is *Oharame Gozen*. Other popular dishes in this area include *Shibazuke*, a purple colored pickle made with egg plants, cucumbers and leaves of the beefsteak plant and seasoned with salt. One noted shop serving this popular dish is Doi Shibazuke Hompo.

MT. HIEI & LAKE BIWA

This section introduces the places of interest, including shrines and temples, dotted around Mt. Hiei and Lake Biwa, Japan's largest lake, in Shiga Prefecture.

WHAT TO SEE

● *MT. HIEI* Mt. Hiei rises 848m close to the boundary between Kyoto and Shiga Prefectures and is a sacred and completely secluded mountain. From its summit you can enjoy splendid views over Kyoto city to the west and Lake Biwa to the east. It can be easily reached by road in an hour from Kyoto city, or in about 30 min. from Lake Biwa.

● *ENRYAKUJI TEMPLE* Easily accessible by cable car, this temple stands in a thick grove of cypress trees at the summit of Mt. Hiei, the highest point on the ridge that separates Kyoto from Lake Biwa. It was established by order of Emperor *Kammu* in 788 by Priest *Saichō*, better-known as *Dengyō-Daishi*, founder of the *Tendai* sect of Buddhism. 1hr. 20 min. by bus from Kyoto Station.

Mt. Hiei became regarded

as a holy place where priests could undergo rigorous training. At the end of the Heian era, Enryakuji Temple was at the peak of its prosperity and there were about 3,000 minor temples on the slopes of the mountain. The temple's powerful army of monks terrorized other Buddhist sects until, in 1571, *Nobunaga Oda* overthrew Enryakuji and destroyed the temple. Today, only 3 pagodas and 120 minor temples remain, in the three areas known as *Tōtō* (East Pagoda), *Saitō* (West Pagoda), and *Yokawa*.

Tōtō *Kompon-Chūdō* is the main hall of Enryakuji Temple. It was frequently destroyed by fire and the present buildings date from 1642. It has a *Tansō* (one-storied) structure and the roof is built in the *Irimoya Zukuri* style (the lower part of the roof forms a trapezoid). The hall features red-painted pillars and galleries with paintings on its ceilings and interesting carvings under the eaves. In its dark, mysterious interior, an image of *Yakushi Nyorai* is enshrined. In the building known as *Daikōdō*, there are images of the founders of Buddhist sects and an image of *Dainichi Nyorai*. The *Kaidan-in* is a sacred place where trainees took vows to be Buddhist priests.

Saitō The *Jōgyōdō* and *Hokkedō* are two vermillion-lacquered training halls, connected by passages. The *Tempōrindō* (also known as *Shakadō*) is the oldest building in the temple grounds and was constructed during the Kamakura era.

Yokawa In this area, 4km. away from *Saitō*, stands *Yokawa-Chūdō*, a large training hall where trainees studied in complete isolation from the distractions of the outside world.

● **LAKE BIWA** This is the largest freshwater lake in Japan with a circumference of 235.2km. The lake takes its name from the *biwa*, a musical instrument, the shape of which the lake resembles. Geologists think the lake was formed by land subsidence. Traditionally, however, it was thought to have been for-

Enryakuji Temple

75

Biwako Ōhashi Bridge

med overnight as the result of an earthquake, which produced Mt. Fuji at the same time. The entrance to Lake Biwa is Ōtsu and Maibara. Regular sightseeing cruises leave Ōtsu for the many scenic spots and resorts on the lakeshore. A round-trip takes about 6 hours.

● **BIWAKO ŌHASHI** This is a toll bridge, 1,350m long, spanning the narrowest point from east to west over Lake Biwa. There is an observation platform in the center of the bridge. From Katata Station on the Kosei line, 5 min. by bus to Biwako Ōhashi stop.

● **BIWAKO BUNKAKAN (CULTURE HALL)** This building is constructed in the shape of a Japanese castle and has a 41m high concrete donjon, which provides good views of Lake Biwa and the surrounding mountains. It contains an aquarium with over 60 varieties of fresh-water fish from Lake Biwa. There is also a museum which exhibits Buddhist images and artifacts and an art gallery. From J.R. Ōtsu Station, 15 min. walk.

● **ŌTSU CITY** Ōtsu is the seat of the Shiga Prefectural Government and the city is beautifully situated on the southwest shore of Lake Biwa. Ōtsu was the home of the imperial court in the 2nd and 7th centuries and the city has preserved many places of historical and cultural importance. 10 min. by train from Kyoto Station. 11km. by car from Kyoto City.

● **MIIDERA TEMPLE** Miidera is the popular name given to Onjōji Temple. It is the headquarters of the *Tendai-Jimon* sect and was founded in 764 in memory of Emperor *Kōbun*. The temple stands in a thick grove of trees on the hillside and in its most prosperous days had 850 buildings in its vast compound. Today it still contains more than 60 structures. The temple houses a bell, popularly called *Benkei-no-hikizurigane*. According to an old tale, *Benkei* was dragging the bell up Mt. Hiei during a battle when he heard the bell tolling, as if it were pleading to be returned. So, *Benkei* returned the bell to its former place at the temple. The tomb of Ernest Francisco Fenollosa, an American art critic, lies in the cemetery of *Hōmyōin* Temple, an annex of Miidera Temple. Fenollosa came to Japan in 1879 and taught at Tokyo University until 1885. Get off the bus at Hama-Ōtsu, walk 4 min.

● *ISHIYAMADERA TEMPLE*
Founded in the 8th C by *Roben*, a famous priest of the Nara era (8th C), this temple was rebuilt twice—once in the 12th C and again near the end of the 16th C. It is known for the beautiful rocks in its grounds, which gave the temple its name, "Stony Hill". Its well-known buildings include the main hall, *Tōdaimon* Gate, *Tahōtō* Pagoda and *Tsukimitei* Pavilion. Attached to the main hall is a building called the *Genji-no-ma* (Hall of Genji). It is here that *Murasaki Shikibu* is said to have written her classic romance, 'The Tale of Genji'. The temple grounds

ŌTSUKYO

In 667, a year after Emperor *Tenji* ascended the throne, the capital was moved from Asuka in Nara to Ōtsu in Shiga. The Emperor set about implementing new rules and regulations and for 5 short years, Ōtsu prospered as the center of administration. However, the citizens were unhappy about the transfer of power to Kyoto and lamented the changes in their lives. This concern can be seen from poems written during the period. The Emperor's active administration implemented the first laws (*Ryō*) and established a register system. However, he died just 4 years after the move to Ōtsu and the capital Nara after a struggle for the throne.

afford a splendid view of the lake, especially on moonlit nights. From Hama-Ōtsu, 15min. on the Keihan Electric Railway to Ishiyamadera Station, then 10 min. walk.

Ishiyamadera Temple

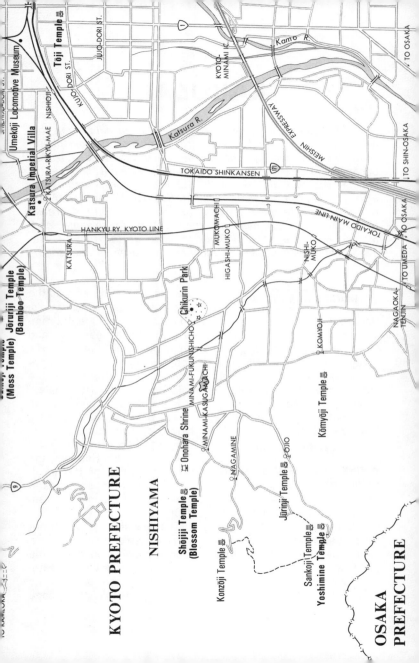

KYOTO PREFECTURE

NISHIYAMA

Tōji Temple 卍

JUJO-DORI ST.

KUJO-DORI ST.

Umekōji Locomotive Museum

Katsura Imperial Villa

KATSURA-RKYU-MAE

NISHIHOJI

Katsura R.

Kamo R.

KYOTO-MINAMI I.C.

MEISHIN EXPRESSWAY

TO OSAKA

TO SHIN-OSAKA

TOKAIDO SHINKANSEN

HANKYU RY. KYOTO LINE

KATSURA

MUKOMACHI

MUKO

HIGASHI-MUKO

NISHI-MUKO

TOKAIDO MAIN LINE

TO OSAKA

TO UMEDA

NAGAOKA-TENJIN

KOMYOJI

TO OSAKA

Jōrurōji Temple 卍
(Bamboo Temple)

(Moss Temple)

Chikurin Park

Onohara Shrine ⛩

MINAMI-FUKUNSHICHO

MINAMI-KASUGAMACHI

Shōjiji Temple 卍
(Blossom Temple)

NAGAMINE

OIO

Kōmyōji Temple 卍

Konzōji Temple 卍

Jūrinji Temple 卍

Sankōji Temple 卍

Yoshimine Temple 卍

OSAKA PREFECTURE

洛 西

RAKUSAI

The Rakusai area covers the gently sloping hills along the west of central Kyoto. The area's peaceful atmosphere attracted the nobility during the Heian era and Rakusai became the site of their villas and devotional temples. A popular sightseeing area with beautiful natural scenery, it also provides a valuable link in Kyoto's history with its Kamakura era temples. Rakusai can be divided into 4 areas: Hanazono and Uzumasa in the center; Arashiyama and Matsuo near the Katsura River; Sagano at the foot of Mt. Takao; and Nishiyama, the mountainous area in the southwest.

HANAZONO & UZUMASA

Hanazono is a busy sightseeing area, boasting many notable temples including Kinkakuji, Ryōanji and Nin-naji. Uzumasa is equally well known—the oldest temple in Kyoto is located here, along with burial mounds dating from the 7th C.

WHAT TO SEE

● *KINKAKUJI TEMPLE (GOLD PAVILION)* Kinkakuji is the popular name given to *Rokuonji* Temple belonging to the Shōkokuji school of the *Rinzai* sect. Set in a beautiful landscape garden at the foot of Kinugasa Hill, it was originally designed as a villa for a court noble in the Muromachi era. Its second owner was the third *Ashikaga shōgun, Yoshimitsu,* who greatly improved its appearance and built the Gold Pavilion. His son, complying with his father's will, later turned the villa into a Buddhist temple.

Most of the original structures were repeatedly destroyed by fire, culminating in the loss of the treasured Gold Pavilion in 1950. However, the present replica of the pavilion, built in 1955, succeeds in preserving the temple's grandeur.

The pavilion is a three-storied structure with a bronze phoenix on top of the roof. Gold leaf covers its exterior, giving the pavilion its name. The temple's landscape garden is attributed to Priest *Soseki* and is one of the finest of its kind in Japan. It includes a brook running into a small lake which is bordered with a grove of maples. Up a zigzagging path beside the brook is an arbor called the *Sekkatei*, built in the time of Emperor *Gomizuno-o* and renovated in 1874. The stone lantern, basin and seat here were brought from the *shō-gun*'s *Muromachi* Palace. Outside the rear gate of the temple stands a temple dedicated to *Fudō-Myō-ō* and his attendants. Get off the bus at Kinkakuji-mae.

Ryōanji Temple

● **RYŌANJI TEMPLE** Founded in 1450, Ryōanji belongs to the *Rinzai* sect and is best known for its rock garden which depicts the sea and a group of islands. The garden is believed to have been arranged in the Muromachi era by *Sōami*, who was greatly influenced by *Zen* philosophy, though some historians hold that it was actually laid out in the Edo era. Regardless of when it was designed, it still remains the best example of the *hiraniwa* (a flat garden devoid of hills or ponds) in the country. The garden is an oblong of sand and skilfully placed rocks and it has a striking simplicity and purity stemming from the principles followed in *Zen* meditation. Get off the bus at Ryōanji-mae.

● **MYŌSHINJI TEMPLE** One of the main temples of the *Rinzai* sect, Myōshinji was founded in 1342 on the site of a villa belonging to Emperor *Hanazono*, but the present buildings are of a later date. The temple has an extremely elaborate layout and contains 47 *tatchū* (minor temples) most housing works of art, as well as the *Sammon* (Main Gate) and various halls. Of the 47 minor temples, however, only three — *Taizō-in*, *Keishun-in* and *Daishin-in*— are open to the public.

The ceiling of the 'Hattō' (lecture hall) is decorated with the huge painting 'Unryū-zu' (Dragon in the Clouds) by *Tan-yū Kanō*. The 'Shōrō'

81

(belfry) contains Japan's oldest bell, cast in 698. The *Sammon* (Main Gate) was built in 1599. It is a massive 2-storied structure, considered a masterpiece of Momoyama style architecture. The upper floor contains a group of Buddhas and has a ceiling painted with dragons and heavenly beings in rich colors.

Taizōin, one of the minor temples, has a well-known *Karesansui* (dry landscape garden) depicting a waterfall and islands. Get off the bus at Myōshinji-mae, walk 2 min. north.

● *NIN-NAJI TEMPLE* Nin-naji is the *Omuro* school headquarters of the *Shingon* sect. Built in 888, there were originally around 60 buildings and the oldest remaining buildings date from the early 17th C.

The temple always had an imperial prince as its superior until 1868. The most notable structures are the five-story pagoda, built in 1637, and the main hall, which contains a wooden statue of Amitabha. The temple grounds contain a unique grove of cherry trees called *'Omuro-no-Sakura'*. These old trees have short thick trunks and bear multiple-petaled blossoms, making the temple a popular attraction in the spring. Get off the bus at Omuro-Ninnaji.

● *KŌRYŪJI TEMPLE* Kōryūji, west of Myōshinji, was founded in 622 for the repose of the soul of Prince *Shōtoku* of *Uzumasa*. It is one of Japan's oldest temples and although the main hall was reconstructed in 1165, most of the Buddha statues it houses were carved in the 7th and 8th centuries. The halls contain over 50 statues, most of which are National Treasures. One statue in particular has historically attracted a lot of devotees — the *'Miroku Bosatsu'*, with its mild pensive expression, ranks among the best figures from this period. In 1960, a college student was so overcome by its beauty that he unthinkingly embraced it and broke off the statue's little finger. Get off the bus at

Nin-naji Temple

82

Movie Village

Kōryūji-mae.

● ***MOVIE VILLAGE*** The village contains a large outdoor set representing a section of a typical feudal town complete with watchtowers and bridges. There are over 20 types of outdoor and indoor sets, most of which are in continuous use, generally for the making of *Jidai geki* (samurai dramas). The village is open to the public and the visitor may see popular movie and T.V. stars strolling along the street in feudal costume. The **Film Art Hall** in the village displays miniature sets of castles, houses, shops and other buildings needed for staging street scenes in various films. A brief history of the Japanese film industry can also be studied here. Get off the bus at Kōryūji-mae, walk 5 min.

● ***NIHON SHISHŪ YAKATA*** Displayed here are over 1,500 beautiful embroidery works as well as ancient Chinese masterpieces and exhibits of Kyoto's folk crafts. Visitors can purchase exquisitely embroidered *kimonos* and carpets. Get off the bus at Nishi-kyōgoku, walk 10 min.

ARASHIYAMA & MATSUO

Arashiyama, with its beautiful natural scenery, and Matsuo, the site of Saihōji Temple, are located along the upper reaches of the Katsura River. Rich landscape dotted with temples makes these areas two of Kyoto's most interesting sightseeing areas.

WHAT TO SEE

83

● ***ARASHIYAMA HILL*** This is the area around *Togetsu-kyō* Bridge which spans the Ōi River, the name given to the middle part of the Hozu River. Arashiyama, at 375m, is more of a hill than a mountain and is covered with pines, interspersed with mountain cherry and maple trees. The beauty of its scenery has long been celebrated in poems and songs and Arashiyama is a very popular place for viewing cherry-blossom in spring, the fresh verdure in early summer and the scarlet maple leaves

Togetsu-Kyo Bridge

in autumn. An interesting trip to make from Kyoto is to shoot the rapids of the Hozu River to Arashiyama, a 2hr. trip covering about 16km. This excursion, in flat-bottomed boats, is especially delightful in spring and equally attractive in summer and autumn.

● *TENRYŪJI TEMPLE* This is the headquarters of the *Tenryūji* school of the *Rinzai* sect and it ranks foremost among the Five Great *Zen* Temples of Kyoto. It was founded in 1339 by the first *Ashikaga* shōgun, *Takauji*, in memory of Emperor *Godaigo*. The temple was repeatedly destroyed by fire and the present buildings date from the late 19th C. At the rear of the abbot's quarters is a noted landscape garden, regarded as a fine example of gardens from the Muromachi era. A large garden, it includes a pond dotted with islets and a dry waterfall built with boulders and rocks. 3min. walk from Arashiyama Station, Keifuku Electric Railway.

● *TOGETSU-KYO BRIDGE* This bridge, which spans the river Ōi, was named by Emperor *Kameyama* and "Togetsu" means "the bridge the moon passes over", since *Kameyama* imagined the moon describing an arc over the bridge. The present bridge was rebuilt in 1934 using steel, but faithfully copies the original structure and blends well with its beautiful surroundings. 2min. walk south of Arashiyama Station.

● *MATSUNO-O SHRINE* This ancient shrine, located at the foot of Mt. Matsuo, is the site of some historical festivals such as the *Matsuno-o* Festival at the end of April, the *Onda* Festival in July and the *Hassaku* Festival in September. These festivals are dedicated to the patron deities of water and *sake* brewing enshrined here and to rice planting. At any time of the year visitors can see casks of *sake* stacked near the shrine and rice spatulas placed in the wire-netting in the grounds. 2min. walk west of Matsuo Station, Hankyū Electric Railway.

● **SAIHŌJI TEMPLE (MOSS TEMPLE)** Saihōji was reputedly founded in the Nara era and later reconstructed in 1339 by *Musō Kokushi*, a distinguished *Zen* priest, who also laid out the temple's magnificent garden. The garden's lower level is a typical example of a "strolling" garden with a large pond and two moss-covered islets symbolizing *Hōrai* (Buddhist paradise). The upper level is a *Karesansui* (dry landscape rock garden), said to be the oldest of its kind in Japan. The entire lower level is covered with over 100 varieties of green and yellow moss—hence the temple is better known as *Kokedera* (Moss Temple). The growth of the moss is attributed to neglect and desolation of the temple during periods of civil war and floods of the river.

To enter the temple, visitors must secure written permission from the Temple Office by sending a return address postcard which includes name, address, age and occupation. This must reach the temple at least 5 days prior to the visit and applications are accepted up to 3 months beforehand. Visitors will obtain permission to enter providing they agree to join in various religious rites such as writing of sutras and listening to sutra readings. These rites usually last about 2 hours. Get off the bus at Kokedera.

● **KEGONJI TEMPLE** Kegonji features an interesting rock garden and also offers good views of Mt. Higashiyama. The temple is popularly called "*Suzumushi* Temple" for the delicate chirp of thousands of *suzumushi*, a "bell ring" insect kept by the priests here. Get off the bus at Kokedera, walk 3min.

● **JIZŌIN TEMPLE (BAMBOO TEMPLE)** Jizōin is also known as *Take-no-Tera* (Bamboo Temple) for the bamboo lining the approach to the temple. Jizōin, which belongs to the *Rinzai* sect, was built in 1367 but was destroyed during a civil war. The Main Hall, Supe-

85

Saihōji Temple

rior's chamber and warehouse were later reconstructed. The grounds contain a flat dry landscape garden called *Jūrokurakan* (16 virtuous priests' garden) featuring rocks arranged on a carpet of moss. Get off the bus at Kokedera, walk 3min. south.

SAGANO

The quiet, serene atmosphere of Sagano was favored by the nobility for their temples and villas. It also attracted many hermits, writers and retired persons. Many literary works have centered around the Sagano area, and one of the most famous of these is the *Heike Monogatari*, which chronicles the rise and fall of the *Heike* family, a powerful *samurai* clan of the 12th C. Sagano and the area around Mt. Takao, north of Sagano have witnessed numerous events of historical significance and are popular sightseeing areas today.

WHAT TO SEE

● *JŌJAKKŌJI TEMPLE* Located on the side of Mt. Ogura overlooking the Sagano area, this temple belongs to the *Nichiren* sect. A steep flight of stairs starts from the thatch-roofed Deva gate and leads up to the Main Hall, *Myōken-*

Rakushisha

dō Hall and *Tahō-tō*. 15min. walk north of Tenryūji Temple.
● *RAKUSHISHA* This is an old hermitage, situated alongside rice fields. The name *Rakushisha*, carved on a stone at the left of the gate, means 'fallen persimmons' and originates from a story that tells of how all the persimmons were blown off the trees on a stormy night. At the rear of the hermitage is the grave of the famous *haiku* poet, *Mukai Kyorai*, who lived here in the Edo era. 3min. walk from Jōjakkōji Temple.
● *GIŌJI TEMPLE* The dancer *Giō*, the lover of the *Heike* family's supreme commander *Taira-no-Kiyomori*, retreated to this temple to live in seclusion after her position had been usurped by another dancer of equivalent rank, *Hotoke Gozen*. It is said that

Hotoke Gozen subsequently realized the futility of her rise in status and joined *Giō* here to spend her days making devotions to Buddha. Their graves lie beside the stone pagoda they erected to the memory of *Taira-no-Kiyomori* on his death. 10min. walk from Rakushi-sha.

● *SEIRYŌJI TEMPLE* Seiryōji was once the mountain villa of Prince *Minamoto-no-Tōru*, son of Emperor *Saga*. Its main buildings are the Main Hall on the path from the Deva Gate, the Amitabha Hall and the *Kyōzō* (sutra storehouses). The temple is commonly called *Shakadō* (Buddha Hall), because of the sandalwood statue of Buddha enshrined in the main hall. It is believed to have been carved by a noted Hindu sculptor and brought to Japan from China during the Sung Dynasty. Get off the bus at Sagashakadō-mae.

● *NEMBUTSUJI TEMPLE* The temple is located in Adashino, an area which means 'place of sadness'. The temple is known as *Adashino Nembutsuji* and in olden times the bodies of those who died without friends or relatives were left here unburied. Over 8,000 stone Buddhas and pagodas have been erected in prayer for the repose of

their souls. The scene presented by these Buddha statues is said to resemble the dry bed of the *River Sai*, the river that divides this world from Hell. An evening memorial service is held here on August 23 and 24, in which lighted candles are placed on the statues to comfort the souls who have no descendants to welcome them when they return to this world during the *Bon* period. 15min. walk north of Giōji.

● *DAIKAKUJI TEMPLE* Daikakuji was originally a villa belonging to Emperor *Saga*, but was converted into a temple in 876 by Emperor *Jun-na*, who appointed a prince as its founder and abbot. The main objects of worship are the wooden statues of *Godai Myō-ō* (Five Vidyrajas), attributed to *Kōbō-Daishi* and

87

Daikakuji Temple

the temple contains many excellent paintings by master artists of the *Kanō* school. The temple stands to the left of Ōsawa pond, traditionally a celebrated place for viewing the autumn moon. The garden, formerly the garden of the imperial villa, is one of the oldest in Japan. It is said to have been designed along the lines of Lake Dongtinghu in China and it offers a splendid view of the Arashiyama hills. Get off the bus at Daikakuji.

● *SAMBI* *Sambi* covers the areas known as Makino-o and Togano-o which lie in a ravine in the mountainous region north of Takao. These places and the area surrounding the **Arashiyama Takao Parkway** (connected to *Shūzan* Road) attract many hikers and sightseers, especially in the autumn when the hillsides are ablaze with color.

● *JINGOJI TEMPLE* Located on the eastern slopes of Mt. Takao, Jingoji Temple belongs to the *Shingon* sect. It was founded in 781 and fell into ruin until it was reconstructed in the 12th C. Jingoji Temple is reached by crossing a bridge over the Kiyotaki River and climbing a long steep flight of old uneven steps. The Study House and belfry stand in a grove of maples and pines. The belfry is a National Treasure and contains a large copper bell, cast in 875, which is one of the 3 noted bells in Japan. Other temple treasures include an image of *Yakushi Nyorai*, a masterpiece from the Heian era and the richly colored statues of *Godai-kokūzō* (Five wise and merciful saints). The view from the temple, looking down

---

KITAYAMA SUGI (CRYPTOMERIA)

Heading north along the Shūzan Road from Togano-o, visitors will come across groves of *Kitayama sugi*, a kind of cryptomeria. Culivation of these trees started in the Muromachi era when Kitayama sugi timber — smooth and free from knots — was favored for the construction of tea ceremony rooms. These slow-growing trees used to be raised in plots and tended carefully before being replanted and the lower branches were cut off to produce smooth, clean timber.

Jingoji Temple

the ravine to the river, is
especially magnificent in
autumn. Get off the bus at
Takao, 20 min. walk.
● **KŌZANJI TEMPLE** Kōzanji
was founded by a priest,
Meikei Shōnin, as a temple
for the *Kegon* sect in 1206
and the temple now belongs
to the *Shingon* sect. The path
on the approach to the temple
is lined with maple and
cryptomeria trees, and contains unique rhombic paving
stones. Among its treasures,
the temple owns a set of four
famous scroll paintings in
black ink known as *Chōjū-
jimbutsu-giga*. The sketches
depict animals playing sports
and games in a humorous
fashion. The temple grounds
contain a tea-ceremony garden believed to be the oldest

in Japan. Get off the bus at
Togano-o, 5 min. walk.

NISHIYAMA

Nishiyama is to the southwest
of central Kyoto and is somewhat off the beaten track,
making it a quiet peaceful
place to sightsee.

WHAT TO SEE

● **KATSURA IMPERIAL VILLA**
This world-renowned villa is
situated between the Katsura
River and the Nishiyama Hills.
Its enormous garden is a
masterpiece of Japanese
landscape gardening which
combines all the different
styles of the period and contains various halls and tea
arbors.

Construction of the villa
was started in the 17th C by
Prince *Toshihito* and took
some 35 years. At the center
of the garden facing the pond
is a cluster of buildings making up the *Shoin* (study halls).
The *Ko-shoin* (old study hall)
features a porch designed for
viewing the moon reflected in
the pond. The *Naka-shoin*
(middle study hall) contains
three apartments and is noted
for its many valuable paintings. The *Shōkin-tei* teahouse
faces the pond on three sides
and was used as a summer
villa. It features a vivid

89

checkerboard design on its sliding paper doors and is also known for its *Yatsumado* (Eight Windows).The North Garden seen from here is considered one of the Imperial Villa's most beautiful views. 'Shōka-tei' is another small teahouse set on a high point and commands a great view of the entire gardens. The country-style building called *Shōi-ken* is one of the largest in the grounds and it has interesting stone lanterns in its garden. All the gardens and buildings are painstakingly designed, with attention paid to the smallest details and the whole effect is of novelty and regularity coexisting harmoniously.

Visitors must secure advance permission from the Kyoto Office of the Imperial Household Agency in the Kyoto Imperial Palace. 15min. walk northeast of Katsura Station.

●**SHŌJIJI TEMPLE** Shōjiji Temple is also known as *Hana-no-Tera* (Blossom Temple) since in spring it is hidden by 450 cherry trees in full bloom. The literary minded priest *Saigyō*, who compiled an anthology of Japanese poems, lived here as a recluse. In the Treasury Hall, near the Main Hall, many

Yoshimine Temple

works of art are preserved, including an image of *Yakushi Nyorai*, the *Nyoirin Kannon-Hanka* and several statues of Buddha. Get off the bus at Minami-Kasugachō, 20min. walk.

● **YOSHIMINE TEMPLE** The temple was founded in 1209 by *Gensan Shōnin* and though destroyed in a later civil war, was reconstructed in the Edo era. The approach to the temple is up a steep slope to the Deva Gate and the main buildings stand hidden in a thick grove of cryptomerias. The temple buildings include the *Tahō-tō*, *Yakushi-dō* and *Kyōzō*. The temple is known for a pine tree called *Yūryū-no-matsu* which resembles a dragon moving about. It stands about 2.6m high with branches extending about 20m. from left to right. From

Higashimukō Station, 20min. by bus then 40min. walk southwest.

● **KŌMYŌJI TEMPLE** This temple stands on the slopes of Mt. Torigamine among pine and cherry trees and maples which are a blaze of color in autumn. It was here that Priest *Hōnen*, founder of the *Jōdo* sect of Amida Buddhism, advocated his doctrine. The main buildings are the Main Hall and *Amida* (Amitabha) Hall which are connected by a corridor. 8min. by bus from Nagaoka Tenjin Station.

SHOPPING & DINING

● **NISHIKI** A restaurant serving traditional Kyoto cuisine. One specialty is *Ōshukuzen*, seasonal dishes served on lacquered trays.

● **KIRISOBA** Recommended at this noodle shop are *Kirisoba* and *Yamakake-soba* (noodles with grated yam). Also excellent is *soba-yu* a hot soup of the water used to cook the noodles, served with various condiments.

● **BODEGON** Bodegon is a kind of Spanish pub, and this establishment imported all its utensils and ornaments from Spain which, together with a splendid decor, helps give it an authentic atmosphere.

● **KICCHŌ** In a pleasant setting in Arashiyama, this refined restaurant is a branch of the prestigious Ōsaka restaurant whose master created a whole new style of Japanese cuisine. It features seasonal dishes artfully presented on elegant tableware.

● **HIROKAWA** This restaurant serves fresh, lightly broiled eels, flavored with a special sauce.

● **MORIKA** This is a famous *tōfu* (bean curd) shop where you can dine or buy to take out. The best water in Sagano is used to produce high quality *tōfu* which is bought by most temples and *tōfu* restaurants in the area. Their specialty is *karashi* (mustard) *tōfu*.

● **ISHIKAWA TAKE-NO-MISE** This bamboo workshop, diagonally opposite Tenryūji Temple, sells all kinds of bamboo products from ear cleaners and toys to instruments for the tea ceremony and bamboo flower arrangements. Also sold are finely crafted masks in the *Saga* style, created by a famous mask artist.

● **SAGA NINGYO-NO-MISE** Located near the gate of Rakushisha Temple, this store sells clay dolls including white snow rabbit dolls and goblin masks in the unique *Uzumasa* style.

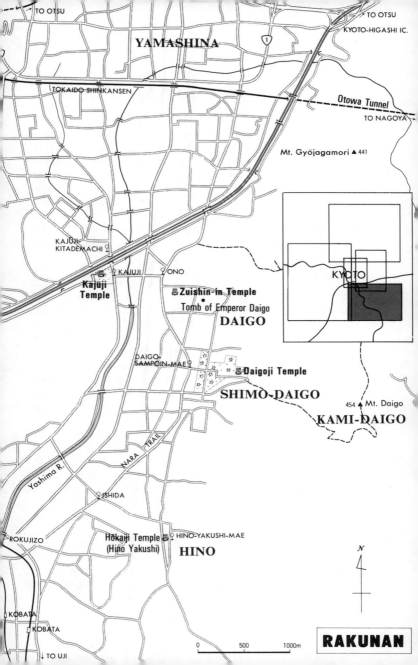

TO OTSU

YAMASHINA

TO OTSU
KYOTO-HIGASHI IC.

TOKAIDO SHINKANSEN

Otowa Tunnel

TO NAGOYA

Mt. Gyōjagamori ▲ 441

KYOTO

KAJŪJI-
KITADEMACHI

KAJUJI

ONO

Kajūji
Temple

🏯 Zuishin-in Temple

Tomb of Emperor Daigo

DAIGO

DAIGO-
SAMPOIN-MAE

🏯 Daigoji Temple

SHIMO-DAIGO

454 ▲ Mt. Daigo

KAMI-DAIGO

NARA TRAIL

Yashima R.

ISHIDA

ROKUJIZO

Hōkaiji Temple 🏯 ○ HINO-YAKUSHI-MAE
(Hino Yakushi)

HINO

N

KOBATA

KOBATA

TO UJI

0   500   1000m

RAKUNAN

RAKUNAN

Rakunan, the south side of the city, is the area around the road linking Kyoto with Nara. It prospered from the very earliest days of Kyoto's history and is noted for the many interesting temples and shrines dotting the area. Although its places of interest are rather scattered, Rakunan contains many important sites and structures from the Heian era including the spectacular Byōdōin Temple at Uji, an area that was once a resort for the wealthy and powerful of Kyoto. It is also a well-known sake-producing and tea-growing district.

WHAT TO SEE

● *SEN-NYŪJI TEMPLE* Sen-nyūji Temple served as the mortuary of the emperors for six centuries after the reign of *Shijō* in the 13th C and the temple grounds contain many imperial tombs. Most of the present buildings date from 1668, however, the *Shariden* (Hall of Sacred Ashes) which had been part of the Imperial Palace, was moved here in 1714. The ceiling of the *Shariden* is adorned with a painting of a dragon, known as *Nakiryū*, (Crying Dragon) since when a person standing below claps, the echo sounds as if the dragon is a emitting a cry.

The *Kannon* Hall houses the *Yōkihi Kannon* (Goddess of Mercy) statue, the model for which is believed to be the wife of Emperor *Gensō* of the Chinese T'ang Dynasty. Get off the bus at Sennyūji-michi.

● *TŌFUKUJI TEMPLE* One of the *Rinzai* sect's main temples, Tōfukuji Temple was built over a period of 19 years, starting in 1236. It consists of 37 buildings in extensive grounds and the huge *Sammon* gate is one of the most important *Zen*-style gates in Japan. The temple is an excellent example of medieval architecture and its location outside the center of Kyoto saved it from the fires that destroyed most of the old capital.

In the temple grounds, a stream called *Sengyokukan* flows through a narrow ravine spanned by 3 bridges. The most famous of the three is

Tsūten-kyō Bridge, known for the beauty of its surroundings when the leaves of the trees change color. A view of *Tsūten-kyō* Bridge can be had from the north of *Hassō* Gardens, a checkerboard patterned garden. Get off the bus at Tōfukuji.

● *FUSHIMI* Fushimi was a very important place after *Hideyoshi Toyotomi* constructed his castle here in 1594. However, after his death in 1598, the magnificent citadel was demolished in 1620 by *Ieyasu Tokugawa*. Today Fushimi is better-known as the site of the *Inari* Shrine. The town also contains many old *sake* cellars since it is an old brewing area.

● *FUSHIMI INARI SHRINE* Since ancient times, Japanese farmers have believed the fox to be the messenger of the god of harvests and there are around 40,000 shrines dedicated to *Inari*, the fox deity. Fushimi-Inari Shrine consists of five shrines on the slopes of Mt. Inari and is the most important of the *Inari* shrines and the focus of this popular belief.

The shrine is actually devoted to five Shintō deities, including the Goddess of Rice and Food. The central struc-

Fushimi Inari Shrine

ture, roofed with cypress bark, is a reconstruction dating from 1949 and its architectural style is characteristic of the later Muromachi period.

A unique feature of the shrine is the 10,000 red *torii* (shrine gates), donated by devotees, which line the approach to the shrine. The interesting stone figures of foxes are also donations from devotees. Near Inari Station.

● *FUSHIMI MOMOYAMA CASTLE* This castle was rebuilt in 1964 to help recapture the grandeur of the villa and flower gardens of the old *Fushimi* castle. The castle, which includes a Japanese garden, features a great 6-story donjon. Seasonal and temporary exhibitions are held on the 1st and 2nd floors while a museum of Momoyama era culture is located on the 3rd to 5th floors. The top floor is set aside as an observatory.

5min. by bus from Momoyama Goryō-mae Station.

● *FUSHIMI MOMOYAMA MAUSOLEA* This is the site of the tombs of Emperor *Meiji* and his consort Empress *Shōken*. The mausolea stand on the hill where *Hideyoshi* once built his castle and the enclosures are reached by climbing a flight of stone steps. The most sacred of the enclosures include the burial mound, the place of worship, and the ceremonial court. The burial mound plot is about 8,100sq.m and the tomb at its center is in the shape of a low mound overlaid with 300,000 pieces of natural granite, overlapping each other like the scales of a fish. It is encircled by two stone fences, the inner one has a bronze gate featuring the imperial crest of a golden chrysanthemum. The tomb of Empress *Shōken* is adjacent to that of

Emperor *Meiji*, but is on a smaller scale. 15min. walk northeast of Momoyama Station.

● *TERADAYA* An old paper lantern bearing the name *Terada-ya* marks the entrance to this old *ryokan* (inn). At the end of the Edo era, the reactionary group *Shinsen-gumi* made a surprise attack on a band of young revolutionaries who had assembled here to plot the overthrow of the government, killing many of them. Get off the bus at Chūshojima, walk 2min.

●*KAJŪJI TEMPLE* Originally built in 900, *Kanjūji* was reconstructed in 1682 by the *Tokugawas*. The most distinguished building here is the *Shoin* (Study hall). The impressive paintings on its sliding screens are attributed to *Mitsuoki Tosa*, a well-known 17th C artist. The temple's beautiful garden includes a pond-centered garden and a *Karesansui*. One of the features of the garden is a *'Kanjūji style'* stone lantern which has a roof shaped like an opened umbrella. From Yamashina Station, 15min. by bus to Ono, walk 10min. west.

● *ZUISHIN-IN TEMPLE* The temple buildings date from 1018 with the exception of the

Teradaya

Main Hall, which was reconstructed in 1599. *Ono-no-Komachi*, a beautiful poet of the Heian era is supposed to have lived here. Her dressing case and the mound where she buried love letters from her admirers can still be seen. The temple has a serene atmosphere and its grounds contain numerous *ume* (Japanese apricot) and rhododendron trees. 15min. walk from Kanjūji Temple.

● *DAIGOJI TEMPLE* Founded in 926, Daigoji is a celebrated temple of the *Shingon* sect. Built on the side of a mountain, it consists of the *Kami-Daigo* at the summit and the *Shimo-Daigo* at the base. The temple comprises more than 70 buildings including a 5-story pagoda, built in 951, one of the oldest existing structures in Kyoto.

The low-branched drooping cherry trees (Prunis Pendula) at Daigoji have been celebrated since olden times and it is here that *Hideyoshi Toyotomi* held his famous cherry-blossom party, *Daigo-no-hanami*, on March 15, 1598. In order to hold this extravaganza, he completely rebuilt the temple, which had been burnt down in the civil wars. The party is now re-enacted annually on the second Sunday of April in a parade known as *Taikō Hanami Gyōretsu*. The participants, dressed in costumes of the Momoyama era, stroll through the grounds of the temple.

Sampo-in Temple is a subtemple located at *Shimo-Daigo*, established in 1115 by *Shokaku*, the 14th abbot of Daigoji. Its present buildings, erected by *Hideyoshi*, contain several chambers decorated with paintings by *Sanraku Kanō*. Its landscape garden, with its many artistically arranged stones, was laid out in 1589 by *Hideyoshi* himself and is considered one of the finest in Japan. Get off the bus at Daigo Sampōin-mae.

● *MAMPUKUJI TEMPLE* 97

Mampukuji is better-known as *Ōbaku-san* as it the headquarters of the *Ōbaku Zen* sect. It was established in 1661 by *Ingen*, a Chinese priest. He built it in the style of the Chinese Ming Dynasty and it is one of the few purely Chinese style temples in Japan. The Main Hall was built of teak imported from Thailand and part of the building has no ceiling, exposing the ribs of the roof. This rafter design is called *Jabara-tenjō*, from its resemblence to the belly of a snake. 5min.

walk east of Ōbaku Station.

● **BYŌDŌIN TEMPLE** In the last days of the Heian era, it was widely believed that *Mappō*, the last days of order before the Buddhist Day of Judgement, had arrived. It was thought that after the world had plunged into chaos, 25 *bosatsu* (living Buddhas) would descend from Heaven to save the world. Byōdōin was originally a villa of *Michinaga Fujiwara*, but in the first year of *Mappō*, 1052, it was converted into a monastery and it vividly illustrates the yearning of Buddhists in those days for *Gokuraku*, the Buddhist Heaven.

The temple's main hall, the *Hōō-dō* (Phoenix Hall), was built in 1053 (and now appears on 10 yen coins). The hall is designed to represent a *Hōō*, a mythical Chinese bird, with its wings outspread. The body is represented by the central hall, the wings by the lateral corridors and the tail by the rear corridor. The whole effect is one of amazing architectural symmetry. On the roof of the central hall stand soaring male and female *Hōō*, cast in bronze. The interior is lavishly decorated with elaborate carvings and paintings by master artists which include a seated wooden statue of Amitabha, attributed to *Jōchō*, the famous Buddhist sculptor.

Because of its graceful shape, the large bronze bell in the belfry here is one of the most noted bells in Japan. This National Treasure bears no inscription but features a design, in relief, of heavenly maidens and lions. 15min. walk from Uji Station.

SHOPPING & DINING

Fushimi dolls have the longest history of any dolls in Japan and are sold at **Tanka** and **Hishiya**, two stores near Fushimi Inari Shrine. Fushimi is also known for the quality of its numerous varieties of crude and refined *sake*.

The Uji area boasts a flavorsome and aromatic green tea, known as *Uji-cha*. A famous tea shop in this area is **Kambayashi Shunsho Honten**. For something different, **Mampukuji Temple** serves Chinese-style vegetable cuisine. They accept groups of 4 or more and reservations are necessary.

Souvenir Stores of Rakunan

NARA

❖

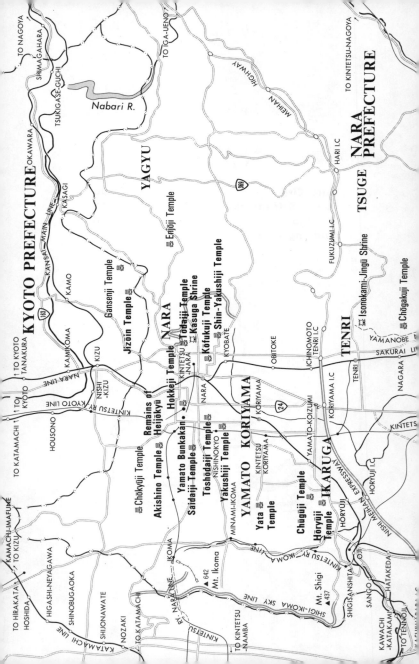

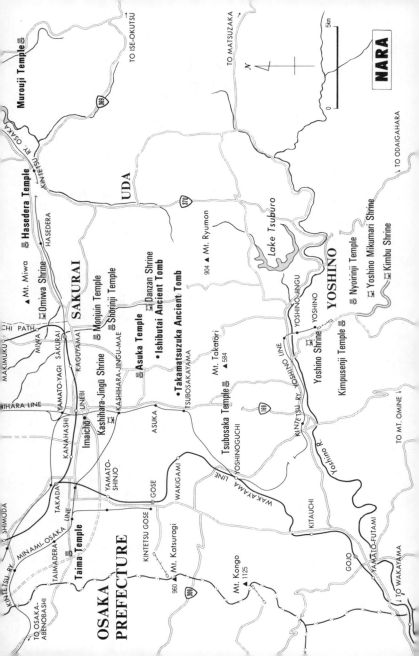

奈 良

NARA

Nara, 40km. south of Kyoto, was the theater of Japan's early history and the cradle of its arts, crafts and literature. Nara has even an older history than Kyoto and was the first national capital between 710 and 794. During this time, Buddhism flourished here under the patronage of the reigning Emperors and the prosperity of this vigorous, progressive Buddhist culture is exemplified by Yakushiji Temple and the magnificent Daibutsu (Great Buddha) in Tōdaiji Temple. Today, Nara is a quiet, pleasant town with an atmosphere of antiquity and ancient culture.

HISTORY

In the early days of Japanese history, it was customary to change the seat of government upon the accession of each ruler. Thus, there was no fixed capital for several centuries until, after administration had become increasingly complicated, Nara was made the first permanent capital in 710 by Empress *Gemmei*. The Nara of 1,200 years ago was a far more extensive city than it is today, with many magnificent palaces and temples. It remained the capital during the reigns of 7 emperors until 794 when Emperor *Kammu* moved the center of administration to Nagaoka in the southwest of Kyoto.

This relatively brief period marked an important epoch in Japanese history. It was marked by the great popularization and growth of Buddhism and the rapid progress of art and industry. Many splendid specimens have been preserved of the arts that flourished in those days, including temple architecture, Buddhist sculpture and painting as well as metalcasting, lacquer-work and embroidery. The period also saw an active relationship maintained with Tang Dynasty China. Numerous official missions were sent there and Buddhist priests visited regularly. This contact with China greatly strengthened the national self-consciousness of the Japanese people.

Nara City

ACCESS

Tokyo to **Nara** Nara is reached in 3hrs 30min. from Tokyo by taking the JR Shinkansen 'Hikari' to Kyoto and transferring to the Kinki Nippon Railway (Kintetsu) limited express for Nara.
Kyoto to **Nara** By Kintetsu limited express: 30min.

By JR Nara Line express: 45min.

Osaka to **Nara** From Namba Station in Osaka on the Kintetsu limited express: 30min.

LOCAL TRANSPORTATION

Although the central attractions at Nara can easily be explored on foot, local transportation is also plentiful. Kintetsu Line and Nara Kōtsū inner-city buses start from JR Nara Station and Kintetsu Nara Station. Nara Kōtsū buses depart every 5 or 10min. and make a circuit of the major sightseeing spots. A 'Free Pass' can be purchased, letting you get on and off these buses at will. Taxis are available from the main railway stations. There are no cruising taxis, however, they can be called from hotels and the like. Rental cars are available at JR Nara Station and rent-a-cycle are available at both main stations.

TOUR HINTS

To see all that Nara has to offer would take the visitor several days. However, since many of the major attractions are grouped in a relatively small area, it is possible to see quite a number of them in a day, by planning your sightseeing routes.

Nara City Course Kintetsu Nara Station—Nara Park—Kōfukuji Temple — Nara National Museum — Tōdaiji Temple — Wakakusayama Hill —Kasuga Shrine—Sasayaki-no-Komichi Path — Shin-Yakushiji Temple — Kintetsu Nara Station.

Nishinokyō and Ikaruga Course Kintetsu Nara Station—Tōshōdaiji Temple — Yakushiji Temple — Remains of Kōriyama Castle—Yatadera Temple—Hōryūji Temple—Chūgūji Temple—Ōji Station.

↑ TO KYOTO

☆ ● **Umanabe Tumuli**

Futaiji Temple 卍

Nara Dreamland

Kōnoike Sports Park

Kombuin Temple 卍

Kōnoike Pond

♀ SAHOYAMA

Mausolea of Emperess Komyo

Mausolea of Emperor Shomu ●

FUTAIJI-GUCHI ♀

KANSAI MAIN LINE

ICHIJO-OJI ST.

(SAHOJI ST.)

← TO HOKKEJI TEMPLE

Saho R.

● **Nara Women's Univ.**

Shōmyōji Temple 卍

← TO NAMBA

SHIN-OMIYA

KINTETSU RY. NARA LINE

KINTETSU-NARA

308

● **Post Office**

NIJO-OJI ST.

Mausolea of Emperor Kaika ●

Shizuka 卍

JR

Kōfukuji Temple

Takemura

🦌 **Five Stori Pogoda**

← TO AMAGATSUJI

SANJO-OJI ST.

Hotel Fujita 🏨

Ikeda Gankodō

NARA

Miyoshino 卍

Sarusawa Pond

Hiraso 卍

Sanjo Pond

Gankōji Temple 卍
(Gokurakubo)

Omori Pond

SAKURAI LINE

✓ TO HORYUJI

TO UNEBI ↓

TO SAKURAI ↓

KYOBATE

NARA CITY

0   500m

N

↑ TO KIZU

• Nara Boy's Prison (396)

Mikasa Hot Springs

MIKASA-ONSENMAE

• Kitayama Jūhachikenkō

Hotel Yamatosansō

NARA OKUYAMA DRIVEWAY

egaimon Gate

Shōsōin Treasure Repository

Wakakusayama
Hill

342 ▲

Daibutsu Pond

Daibutsuden
(Main Hall)

🏯 Nigatsudō
🏯 Sangatsudō

Kaidan-in
Temple

Tōdaiji Temple

⛩ Tamukeyama Shrine

Kagami Pond

Neiraku Art Gallery
ara Prefecture
useum

Isuien
• Garden

🏛 Tōdaiji Office
• Nandaimon Gate
⛩ Mori Narazuke-Ten

ara Prefectural Office

⛩ Himuro Shrine

Nara National
Museum

ational
reasure Hall

♀ NARA-DAIBUTSUMAE

♀ KASUGA-TAISHAMAE

Kasuga Shrine

🏯 Kikusuirou Ryokan

Nara Park

Man-yō Botanical Garden

Araike Pond

🏯 Nara Hotel

Sagiike Pond

⛩ Wakamiya Shrine

♀ FUKUCHIINMACHI

• Imanishike Shoin

Jurin-in Temple

Shin-Yakushiji Temple 🏯

Ichinoi Pond

TO YAGYU

• Nara Univ. of Education

• Nara National Hospital

Noto R.

♀ BYAKUGOJI

Byakugoji Temple

WHAT TO SEE

NARA CITY

Nara is a small city with very scenic surroundings and it has a restful, timeless atmosphere. With its large park, it is a very pleasant place to walk around and admire the ancient temples, shrines, tombs, ruins and many other reminders of the grandeur of the Nara era.

● **NARA PARK** Nara Park covers 5.25sq.km. and contains most of Nara's major attractions including Kasuga Shrine, Kōfukuji and Tōdaiji Temples and Nara National Museum. The park is popularly known as 'Deer Park' since over 1,000 tame deer roam freely here. Cedars, oaks and wisterias cover the park and it has good walking paths and is well signposted. Close to the entrance is Sarusawa Pond,

stocked with carp and turtles and fringed with weeping willows. 10min. walk east of Nara Kintetsu Station: near Kenchō-mae or Hakubutsu-kan-mae bus stops.

● **KŌFUKUJI TEMPLE** Kōfukuji, which stands near Sarusawa Pond, is the headquarters of the *Hossō* sect. It was founded in 710 as the tutelary temple of the *Fujiwara* clan who later held sway from the 9th to 11th centuries. As the influence of the Fujiwaras grew, Kōfukuji expanded in size and importance. Halls and pagodas were added, the grounds were enlarged and at the height of its prosperity, Kōfukuji contained as many as 175 buildings. It flourished as an important center of learning and became one of the 'Seven Great Temples of Nara'. 10min, walk east of Kintetsu Nara Station.

Five-story Pagoda This pagoda, reflected on the surface of nearby Sarusawa Pond, has long been known as one of Nara's most photogenic sights. At 50.8m. high, it is the second tallest in Japan and it contains four Buddhas on its first story. It was first built in 730 and has since been destroyed by fire five times. The present structure dates from 1426 and is an

Nara Park

exact replica of the original.
Tō-Kondō This hall, immediately north of the pagoda, was founded in 726 by Emperor *Shōmu* (701-756) to pray for the welfare of the nation and for the recovery from illness of former Empress *Genshō*. The present building is a reconstruction dating from 1415 and in the main hall the central object of worship is a gilded bronze statue of *Yakushi Nyorai*. It is accompanied by the statues of *Nikkō-Bosatsu*, *Gakkō-Bosatsu* and six of the Twelve Divine Generals.

Chū-Kondō (Central Main Hall) Located to the northwest of Tō-Kondō, this hall was originally built in 710 and later reconstructed in 1819. It houses a wooden statue of Sakyamuni and several other works of art.

Nan-endō Standing southwest of Chū-Kondō, this octagonal hall was established in 813 and was burnt down numerous times. The present reconstruction dates from 1741 and it houses several valuable sculptures, the chief one being the 3.4m gilded wooden image of the *Fukūkensaku Kannon*. This is attributed to *Kōkei*, father of master sculptor *Unkei* and forerunner of the realistic

Kōfukuji Temple

school of sculpture in the Kamakura era (1192-1333). Other statues include the Four Heavenly Guardians trampling demons underfoot and the Six Patriarchs of the *Hosso* Buddhist sect.

Three-story Pagoda This graceful pagoda, 18.4m tall, stands to the southwest of Nan-endō. It was rebuilt in 1148 and is a fine example of Heian era architecture.

Hoku-endō To the north of the Three-story Pagoda, this is another octagonal hall, founded in 721. It has been rebuilt four times and the present hall dates from 1208. It houses a National Treasure, the 1.5m. wooden statue of *Miroku-Bosatsu*, attributed to *Unkei*.

● **TŌDAIJI TEMPLE** Tōdaiji, the grand headquarters of the *Kegon* Buddhist sect, is well-known for the *Daibutsu* , the world's largest bronze statue

107

Tōdaiji Temple Nigatsu-dō

of Buddha. Construction of the temple began in 741 by order of Emperor *Shōmu* and was completed 15 years later. Emperor *Shōmu* conferred on it the highest honor by making it the head of all the *Kokunji* (Provincial Temples), which he had ordered built in each province.

Today, Tōdaiji Temple is Nara's central attraction. Its principal buildings are Nandaimon Gate, Daibutsuden (Hall of the Great Buddha), the Belfry, Sangatsudō and Nigatsudō halls and Tegaimon Gate. 3min. walk north of Nara Daibutsu-mae bus stop.

Nandaimon Gate This is the imposing front entrance to the temple, a reconstruction dating from 1199. It is supported by 18 pillars, each 19m. high and its exterior niches contain two fearsome-looking wooden statues of *Kongō-Rikishi* (Deva Kings), traditional guardians of a Buddhist sanctuary. These 8.4m. high statues are attributed to *Unkei* and *Kaikei*, noted Kamakura era sculptors. The rear niches contain a pair of stone *shishi* (an animal supposed to resemble a lion). They are 1.8m. high and stand on tall stone pedestals in a spirited posture. They were carved in 1196 by a Sung artisan from China and are

---

Omizu-tori Festival

Shunie is the original name of this 1,200 year old fire and water festival, held at Nigatsu-dō Hall in Tōdaiji Temple for the repentance of sins. A highlight of the festival is the exorcism by fire known as *Dattan*, held on Mar. 12—14. In the evenings, monks light large *taimatsu* (pine torches) and wave them around on the outer gallery of Nigatsu-dō, showering the spectators with sparks.

among the few remaining stone works done in the Sung style.

Daibutsuden (Hall of the Great Buddha) This impressive building is the world's largest wooden structure, measuring 57m. long, 50.5m. wide and 47.58m. high. It was burnt down twice and the present reconstruction dates from 1709, built on a scale about 2/3 of its original size. Adorning the ridge of its massive roof are a pair of gilt ornaments, known as *shibi* for their resemblance to the tail of the *Kite* bird.

Daibutsu (Great Buddha) The casting of this gigantic statue was completed in 749. It was partially destroyed in fires and earthquakes and has undergone several restorations—the body was restored in the Kamakura era, the right hand in 1580 and the head was repaired in 1690. The *Daibutsu* represents *Rushana-Butsu* (Buddha Vairocana) in a seated posture and in the act of delivering a sermon. The statue stands 15m. high and weighs 452tons.

Campanile Located east of the Daibutsuden, this sturdy structure dates from the 13th C. and contains Japan's second largest bell, originally cast in 749. It measures 3.9m.

high and the circumference of the base is 8.2m.

Sangatsu-dō The hall's name means 'Third Month Hall' since an annual service is held here in March for the *Hokekyō* Sutra. Founded in 733, it is the oldest of the Tōdaiji structures although the Raidō (Outer Chapel) was added in 1199. It houses a 3.6m statue of *Fukūkenjaku Kannon*, surrounded by 14 smaller statues.

Tegaimon Gate This stands on the western boundary of the temple and forms its northern entrance. The gate is supported by 8 pillars and is characteristic of the robust style of architecture used in the 8th C.

Shōsōin (Treasure Repository) 300m. northwest of Daibutsuden, this building was constructed in the *Azekura* style and resembles a large log

Tōdaiji Temple Daibutsuden

cabin on stilts. It contains numerous priceless art works from the late Nara era as well as the treasures and household utensils of Emperor *Shōmu*. The contents are aired annually during the crisp, dry days in late October. At this time some of the treasures are exhibited at Nara National Museum.

● *WAKAKUSAYAMA HILL*
Extensive views can be enjoyed from the top of this row of three grassy hills. On the evening of Jan. 15 every year, the grass is set alight, making a lively spectacle. Near Nara Daibutsu-mae bus stop.

● *KASUGA SHRINE* This shrine was founded in 768 and is one of the most famous *Shintō* shrines in the country. It was founded as the tutelary shrine of the *Fujiwara* family and actually consists of four shrines, each consecrated to a different *Shintō* deity. It has

a picturesque setting, with the vermilion-lacquered buildings forming a beautiful contrast to the surrounding woods.

At its front entrance near the grounds of Kōfukuji Temple stands the first *torii* (gate), originally built in 836. About 1,600m. further on is the second *torii*. From here a 800m. avenue lined with tall cedars leads to the south gate. Some 1,800 stone lanterns line the approach and are offerings from devotees. These lanterns, along with the 1,000 metal lanterns hanging from the eaves of the shrine corridors, are lit twice a year during the Lantern Festivals.

Inside the south gate is a spacious area containing an old floorless building called the **Heiden**. This hall dates from 1650 and is where offerings are made to the deities. To the left of this is the **Naoraiden** (Entertainment Hall) where various ceremonies take place. From the Heiden a flight of steps leads to the middle gate behind which are four shrines, collectively called the **Honden** (Main Hall). These buildings used to be reconstructed every twenty years, each time with only slight alterations from the original design. The present buildings are thus

Kasuga Shrine

Sasayaki-no-Komichi Path

good examples of shrine architecture from the late 8th C. 15min. walk on the main approach from Kasuga-Taisha-mae bus stop.

● **KASUGA-WAKAMIYA SHRINE**
Situated 190m. from the south gate of Kasuga Shrine, this shrine is famous for its *On-matsuri* festival, which features a parade with people in traditional dress. The approach to the main hall is lined with stone lanterns and in front of the hall stands a low, elongated building divided into three sections. The southern section is the hall where *Kagura* (sacred Shinto dancing) and music are performed.

● **MAN-YO BOTANICAL GAR-DENS** The gardens cover an area of about 1 ha. in the precincts of the Kasuga Shrine and contain over 300 species of plants. These plants were mentioned in the *Man-yō-shū*, the oldest anthology of Japanese poetry, compiled in the Nara era.

● **SASAYAKI-NO-KOMICHI PATH**
This 'lane of whispering' runs for 500m. through the precincts of Kasuga Shrine. It forms a natural tunnel through Japanese andromeda bushes, whose white flowers at the end of March make a pretty sight.

● **SHIN-YAKUSHIJI TEMPLE**
The temple was founded in 745 by Empress *Kōmyō*, consort of Emperor *Shōmu*. The main hall dates from the founding of the temple and contains a seated wooden image of *Yakushi-Nyorai*, carved in the 9th C. This famous statue sits on a circular pedestal, surrounded by twelve exquisite clay images of *Jūni-Shinshō* (The Twelve Divine Generals). Eleven of them are registered as National Treasures. With the exception of the main hall, which typifies the architectural style of the late Nara era, all other structures were reduced to ashes long ago. The gold-bronze image called the *Ko-Yakushi* is a remarkable work of art. Another priceless treasure is a painting of Nirvana from the late Heian era. 10min. walk

Byakugōji Temple

southwest of Kasuga-Wakamiya Shrine.

● **BYAKUGŌJI TEMPLE** The temple stands on the slopes of Mt. Takamado and offers good views over Nara city from the top of the steps leading from the main gate. Originally constructed in the Nara era, it was rebuilt in the Kamakura era by Priest *Eison*, for the common people. The temple enshrines a wooden sculpture of *Amida-Nyorai*. Attractions in the temple's garden include the blooms of the unique camellia, *Goshoku Tsubaki* and pretty bush clover.

● **TŌNO-O STONE STATUES** On the 2km. mountain path that leads from Gansenji Temple to Jōruriji Temple, hikers will come across numerous stone statues. These are the only relics of a medieval temple once standing here and the statues, which have interesting expressive features, include *Warai Botoke*, a Buddhist image wearing a gentle smile and *Karasu-no-tsubo* (Crow's pots). Autumn is a good time to visit, when orange persimmons color the mountains.

● **JŌRURIJI TEMPLE** Jōruriji, also known as Kutaiji, was established in 1047 and became a refuge for aristocrats, who came here for meditation and religious study. The Main Hall contains 9 statues of *Amida-Nyorai* as well as a characteristically plump, painted statue of *Kisshōten*, the goddess of beauty and felicity. Near Jōruriji-mae bus stop.

● **YAGYŪ KAIDŌ ROAD** This mountain road, known as Yagyū Kaidō or Takisakamichi runs northeast alongside the Noto River, from near Shin Yakushiji Temple. This 17km. stone-paved path once led to Yagyū-no-sato, a place where important samurai studied traditional martial arts under the guidance of the *Yagyū* clan. The road to the samurai training camp is now a hiking course, dotted with small stone statues. 10min. walk east of Shin-Yakushiji Temple.

SAHOJI & NISHINOKYŌ

Sahoji lies in the northern part of Nara, around the base of Mt. Nara and Nishinokyō is an outlying rural district. These areas flourished in the 8th C. and the scenery here became a popular subject for poets of that time. There are various sites of historic interest here, including temples and burial mounds.

● *HOKKEJI TEMPLE* Empress *Kōmyō* established Hokkeji in the mid 8th C. as the headquarters of all provincial nunneries. The temple houses a *Jūichimen Kannon* (Eleven Faced Goddess of Mercy). There is a neatly arranged (pond-centered) garden here that is popular when its irises bloom. The *Hinaeshiki* Festival is held here in early April to worship 55 statues of the infant Buddha, which are bedecked with flowers. 5min. walk from Hokkeji-mae bus stop.

● *FUTAIJI TEMPLE* This temple is famous as the place where *Ariwara-no-Narihira*, a grandson of Emperor *Heizei,* once lived during the Heian era. The temple is therefore also known as *Narihira* Temple and is quite grand, in keeping with *Narihira's* status. His stone tomb, built to resemble a ship, lies in the temple's garden where camellias, bush clover and chrysanthemums bloom in season. 5min. walk north of Futaiji-guchi bus stop.

● *UWANABE AND KONABE TUMULI* Lying in the center of ponds, these two enormous tumuli, Uwanabe in the east and Konabe in the west, contain graves of people yet to be identified. The ancient tumuli are keyhole-shaped, with one end square and the other rounded. Uwanabe is 255m. long and Konabe 204m. and both are terraced and covered with pine trees. 5min. walk northwest of Futaiji Temple.

● *REMAINS OF HEIJŌKYŪ* On the flat land spreading out to the west of Hokkeji Temple lie the remains of the former Heijōkyū Palace. From here, 7 successive emperors ruled the nation during the Nara era and the 102ha. site is supposed to contain the remains of the Daikokuden (National Event Hall), the Dairi

113

Futaiji Temple

(Emperor's Residence), Tōgū (Princes' Residence) and the government offices. Excavation and restoration has been taking place here since 1959. 2min. walk west of Heijōkyū-ato bus stop.

● **SAIDAIJI TEMPLE** Founded in 765, the temple is the headquarters of the *Shingon-Ritsu* sect and once ranked in grandeur with Tōdaiji Temple. It had many stately buildings and was one of the 'Seven Great Temples of Nara', however, after numerous fires little remains today. The Shiōdō Hall contains relics from the original temple including bronze and wooden statues of the Four Devas (Guardians) and, beneath them, an impressive copper devil. *Ōchamori*, a special tea ceremony in which tea is drunk from cups larger than a person's head, is held at the temple on the second weekend in April. 5min. walk southwest of Yamato Saidaiji Station on the Kintetsu Line.

● **YAMATO BUNKAKAN** This is a private art gallery with a collection of over 2,000 ancient oriental works of art, including works from mainland Asia. The *"Matsuura Folding Screen"*, a National Treasure, can be seen here. 5min. walk southeast of Gakuen-mae Station on the Kintetsu Line.

● **AKISHINODERA TEMPLE** Founded in 780 by Priest *Zenju*, the temple is well-known for the statue it enshrines of *Gigeiten*, the goddess of success and fortune. It is the only one in Japan and while the head dates back to the Nara era, the rest of the statue is attributed to *Unkei*, master sculptor of the later Kamakura era. The present buildings were reconstructed in the Kamakura era and are excellent examples of the Nara era architectural style. 20min. walk northwest of Yamato-Saidaiji Station on the Kintetsu Line.

● **NARA DREAMLAND** This is a giant amusement park for all ages, situated on Kurokami Hill. Its chief attractions are a doubleloop roller coaster and 120km/h. bobsleighing. Dreamland South Exit bus stop.

● **YAKUSHIJI TEMPLE** The headquarters of the *Hossō* sect, Yakushiji was founded in 680 and was one of the 'Seven Great Temples of Nara'. It is admired for its **Three-story Pagoda**, the only temple building not reconstructed. This elegant pagoda, known as *Tōtō* (Eastern Pagoda), was erected in

730 and stands 33.6m high. It appears to be six-storied since each story has an additional roof-like projection called a *mokoshi*. The *Saitō* (West Pagoda) was reconstructed in 1981 and stands alongside the Tōtō.

Behind the Tōtō is the **Tōindō** (East Hall), built in 1285, which houses a famous bronze statue of *Shōkan-non*, acclaimed as an outstanding example of the artistic skills attained in the Hakuhō era (645-710).

The **Kondō** (Main Hall) houses the celebrated bronze statues of the *Yakushi* Trinity: *Yakushi-Nyorai*, (Nyorai is a person who has experienced truth) and his two attendants, *Nikkō Bosatsu* and *Gakkō Bosatsu*. Near Nishino-kyō Station on the Kintetsu Line.

● **TŌSHŌDAIJI TEMPLE** This great temple is the headquarters of the *Ritsu* sect and was founded in 759 by *Ganjin*,

illustrious Chinese priest of the Tang Dynasty.

Kondō (Main) has survived since the temple's founding and in one of the largest and most beautiful structures remaining from the late Nara era. Its chief statue is the 3.3m. Buddha Vairocana, covered with gold leaf. Its halo was originally decorated with 1,000 small Buddhas, of which some 864 remain. The walls and pillars of the hall were once decorated with 2,000 Sakyamuni, but they cannot be discerned today. The Vairocara statue is surrounded by other wooden statues, all examples of exquisite workmanship. One of these is a Thousand-armed Kannon which differs from other similar statues in that its 42 large and 911 small arms are arranged like a radiant halo.

Kōdō (Lecture Hall) Housing many treasures including the wooden, 2.4m *Miroku Bosatsu*, dating from the 13th C. Although it has undergone several reconstructions, the hall is important as the only remaining example of palace architecture from the Tempyō era (729-749).

Miedō Northeast of the Kōdō, it houses a dry lacquer statue of *Ganjin*, dating from 762, regarded as one of the

Tōshōdaiji Temple

greatest portrait statues in Japan. *Ganjin* was invited to Japan to ordain Japanese Buddhists and introduced the *Ritsu* doctrines to this country. 10min. walk north of Yakushiji Temple.

IKARUGA

This section introduces Ikaruga, in the southwest of Nara, an area significant for the life and administration of Prince *Shōtoku*. It also introduces the castle town of Kōriyama and the Mt. Shigi area.

● **YAMATO-KŌRIYAMA** The castle here was built in the Muromachi era and although other castles in the vicinity were destroyed in the Edo era by the local *shōgun* who feared the Emperor's power, this one was allowed to remain. The area in also known for its red earthernware, *Akahadayaki*. From Nara to Kōriyama Station, 4min. on the Kansai Honsen Line.

● **HŌRYŪJI TEMPLE** The headquarters of the *Shōtoku* sect, Hōryūji is also rich in magnificent architectural and sculptural works of art. It is the oldest existing temple in Japan and one of the most important in Japanese history and art.

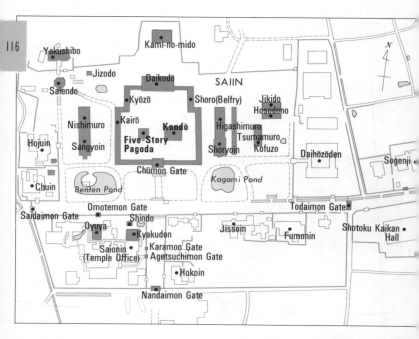

116

Hōryūji was founded in 607 by prince *Shōtoku*, nephew and Regent of Empress *Suiko*. The prince was the most influential national figure of his time and a devoted patron of Buddhism. The temple comprises about 40 buildings and is divided into two sections, the *Saiin* (West Temple) and the *Tōin* (East Temple).

SAIIN This is often regarded by many as Hōryūji Temple itself. probably because the Tōin is located a little distance away in a separate enclosure.

Kondō (Main Hall) This is one of the chief buildings in the

Ikaruga

Saiin and one of the world's oldest buildings. It is double-roofed with tiles and has a *mokoshi*, an extra wooden roof. Several Buddhist statues and other works of art are housed here and the most famous is the bronze *Shaka* Trinity, cast in 623. The central figure is *Shaka* (Gautama Buddha), flanked by two *Bosatsu*, *Yakuō* and *Yakujo*. The Trinity is a valuable masterpiece, representative of sculpture in the Asuka era (552-645).

Five-story Pagoda This stands to the west of the Kondō and was built in typical Asuka style. It is 32m. high and measures 10m. on each side and like other similar structures in Nara, it has a *mokoshi*. It still has the same timber used in its original construction in 607.

Daikōdō (Lecture Hall) To

117

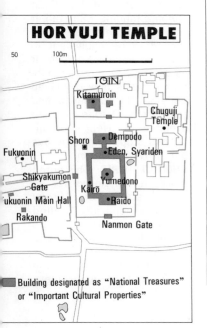

HORYUJI TEMPLE

50   100m

TOIN
Kitamuroin

Chuguji Temple

Shoro   Dempodo

Fukuonin   Eden. Syariden

Shikyakumon Gate   Yumedono

Kairo

ukuonin Main Hall   Raido

Rakando

Nanmon Gate

Building designated as "National Treasures" or "Important Cultural Properties" the north of the pagoda, this contains the gilded wooden figures of the *Yakushi* Trinity: *Yakushi Nyorai* and his two attendants. Originally built in 925, the present hall dates from 990. To the west of the Daikōdō is the *Kyōzō* (Sutra Library) and to the east, the *Shōrō* (Belfry), both of which are National Treasures.

Daihōzōden (Treasure Hall) This was erected in 1940 to house over 1,000 treasures, originally kept in the Kondō. Among these is the Miniature Shrine revered by lady *Tachibana*, mother of Empress *Kōmyō*, containing the bronze *Amida* Trinity. Another National Treasure is the *Tamamushi-no-Zushi*, a small shrine which belonged to Empress *Suiko*.

TŌIN The site of the Tōin was originally Prince *Shōtoku'*s Ikaruga Palace, which he built in 601 and was his residence until his demise in 621. The palace later fell into ruin and was replaced with the Tōin. It was built in 739 by Priest *Gyōshin* under imperial order and was dedicated to Prince *Shōtoku* and his family.

Yumedono(Hall of Dreams) This beautiful octagonal building is the main hall of the Tōin. Prince *Shōtoku* reputedly used the hall for deep meditation whenever he came across passages too difficult to comprehend while annotating Buddhist sutras. The hall houses a strikingly elegant wooden statue of the *Guze Kannon*. Standing 1.8m tall, it is covered in gold leaf and is believed to be equivalent in stature to Prince *Shōtoku*. It was once concealed from public view but is now displayed from April 11 to May 5 and again from October 22 to November 3. Near Hōryūji-mae bus stop, 50min. by bus from JR Nara Station.

● **CHŪGŪJI TEMPLE** This noted nunnery is well-known for its wooden statue of *Miroku Bosatsu* (generally called *Nyoirin Kannon*) which wears a famous benevolent, merciful smile. Among other treasures is a piece of one of the world's oldest embroidery

Hōryūji Temple

works, the *Tenjukoku Shūchō*. Prince *Shōtoku*'s wife ordered it to be made to help the Prince in his life in heaven. It is part of a Mandala showing a scene in the Land of Heavenly Longevity. 8min. walk from Chūgūji-mae bus stop.

●**YATADERA TEMPLE** Built by Emperor *Temmu* in 673, the temple stands halfway up Yata Hill over-looking the Nara basin. At the height of its prosperity there were over 48 minor temples in its grounds, however, only 4 remain today. It enshrines a *Jūichimen* (Eleven-faced) *Kannon* and is also known as *Ajisai* (Hydrangea) Temple for the 4,000 hydrangeas which flower here in June. Near Yatadera-mae bus stop.

●**NARA PREFECTURAL MUSEUM OF FOLK CULTURE** The museum stands on a hill in Kōriyama and it exhibits tools and other items used in daily

Yamanobe-no-michi Path

life in the Nara region from the Edo to Meiji eras. Five model houses from those periods stand in its garden. 10min. walk from Yatadera-mae bus stop.

●**MT. IKOMA & MT. SHIGI** Mt. Ikoma (642m) is the major mountain in the Ikoma area and is the site of Hōzanji Temple and an amusement park. Mt Shigi (437m) lies in the south of the Ikoma area and features many hot springs and Chōgosonshiji Temple,

119

Yamanobe-no-michi Path

Mentioned in ancient documents, this is one of Japan's oldest roads and it runs almost straight for 35km. from Nara, via Tenri, to Sakurai. The path offers a lot of historic sites, including temples, Buddhist stone statues, the ancient tomb of Emperor *Sujin* and Isonokami Shrine. The path is well-signposted and makes an interesting excursion, either as a hike or a cycling trip.

Hasedera Temple

devoted to the god of commerce. The two mountains are linked by the Shigi-Ikoma Skyline Road.

OUTLYING AREAS

Asuka and Yamanobe, in the center of Nara Prefecture, are dotted with the remains of the ancient culture which flourished here, including old temples and tumuli. Hase, Murou and Yoshino are relatively accessible places in these districts, but it is recommended that visitors plan their routes carefully.

● *HASEDERA TEMPLE* Founded in 686, this is the *Buzan* school headquarters of the *Shingon* sect and the 8th of the 33 holy *Kannon* temples for pilgrimage in western districts. The main hall was originally built in 727 by Emperor *Shōmu* and the present recon-

struction, dating from 1650, contains an 8m *Jūichimen* (Eleven faced) *Kannon*. A 195m. corridor with 399 steps leads up to the main building from the Deva Gates. It is divided into 3 sections and has elliptically-shaped lanterns suspended from its ceilings. The temple grounds are at their best in spring when over 7,000 peonies bloom and the numerous cherry trees blossom. 20min. walk from Hasedera Station on the Kintetsu Line.

● *MUROUJI TEMPLE* Murouji, situated in a village near the headwaters of the Murou River, was founded at the end of the Tempyō era (8th C) by Priest *Kenkyō* of Kōfukuji Temple. *Keishōin*, mother of the 5th *Tokugawa shōgun*, helped wrest control of the temple away from Kōfukuji and the temple became known as *Nyonin Kōya* a devout mountain for women. The main attractions here are the **Mirokudō Hall** with its statue of *Shaka Nyorai* and the **Kondō (Golden Hall)** which contains various National Treasures. Rhododendrens bloom in the temple grounds from late April to early May. Take the bus from Murouguchi-ōno Station on the Kintetsu Line to

Murouji-mae bus stop.

● **ASUKAJI** Asuka was the first capital designated by the *Yamato* Court and here the early culture introduced from Korea was reshaped, thus Asuka is referred to as the birthplace of Japanese culture. The ancient road running through here makes a pleasant trip, especially in spring when the roadside is a bloom with flowers.

● **ASUKA TEMPLE** Also known as *Angoin*, this is the oldest full-scale temple in Japan, although very little of it remains today. It was founded by *Soga-no-Umako* of the *Soga* clan, who, next to the Emperors, held political and religious power and was intent on spreading Buddhism. Today, only the foundation stones and the Main Hall remain. A bronze statue of *Shaka Nyorai*, known as the *Asuka Daibutsu* cast in the 6th C, is kept in the Main Hall.

Near Asuka Daibutsu-mae bus stop.

● **ISHIBUTAI ANCIENT TOMB** 30 large stones, together weighing about 75 tons, were used to construct this tomb, the grave of *Soga-no-Umako*. It is a good example of 7th C tombs, with its square base and round top. 15 min. walk southeast of Okadera-mae bus stop.

● **TAKAMATSUZUKA ANCIENT TOMB** Dating from the 7th or 8th century, this is a small circular tomb, 18m. in diameter. In 1972, beautiful frescoes were discovered here and although the inside of the tomb is closed to the public, copies of the frescoes are exhibited in the Takamatsuzuka Fresco Museum. 15min. walk from Asuka Station on the Kintetsu Line.

● **TAIMA TEMPLE** Taima stands at the foot of Mt. Futagami and is known for its east and west towers, the only twin towers remaining from the Tempyō era. The temple's chief treasure is the famous mandala of the Buddhist paradise, the *Taima Mandara*. Legend has it that *Chūjō-hime*, a nun, wove this mandala overnight. A copy of this was made in the Muromachi era and now hangs in the Main Hall. 15min. walk west of

Asuka

Taimadera Station on the Kintetsu Line.

● **YOSHINO** Mt. Yoshino used to be a retreat for ascetic Buddhists and its temples are connected with the names of Emperor *Godaigo* and *Minamotono-Yoshitsune*. Today, it is a well-known site for cherry blossom viewing. Blossoms appear gradually, first on the trees at the base of the mountain, then on those halfway up, followed by the upper hillside and the top. This gradual blossoming is called *Shimo-sembon, Naka-sembon, Kami-sembon* and *Oku-sembon* (*'sembon'* means 1,000 trees) because each of the four groups has around 1,000 trees. 2min. walk to the ropeway station from Yoshino Station on the Kintetsu Line.

WHERE TO EAT

There are a lot of restaurants concentrated around Nara Station. **Shizuka** is a specialty restaurant serving *Kamameshi*, rice dishes using seasonal ingredients. **Hirasō** is an old shop selling the sushi peculiar to Yoshino, *Kaki-no-ha-zushi* in which vinegared rice topped with salted mackerel and salmon is wrapped in persimmon leaves. At **Miyoshino**, the surprise of the *Bikkuri Udon* (Surprise *Udon*) will come from the generous quantity of noodles and the speed with which the dish is served.

WHAT TO BUY

Most souvenirs can be found in the Nara Commerce and Tourist Building near Kintetsu Nara Station. Nara produces most of Japan's *sumi* ink and many old stores along Sanjō-dori Street such as **Kobaien** and **Genrindō** specialize in ink and calligraphy brushes. **Akahadayaki** is the area's solid, chunky pottery. Other local items include fans decorated with traditional pictures. **Ikeda Gankōdō** sell folding fans. Nara's special confectionery, *Aoniyoshi*, made from flour and sugar, can be bought at **Chiyonoya Takemura**. *Narazuke* pickles, pickled in sake lees are a local specialty and are available at the famous store, **Mori Narazuketen**.

Mt. Yoshino

OSAKA·KOBE

❖

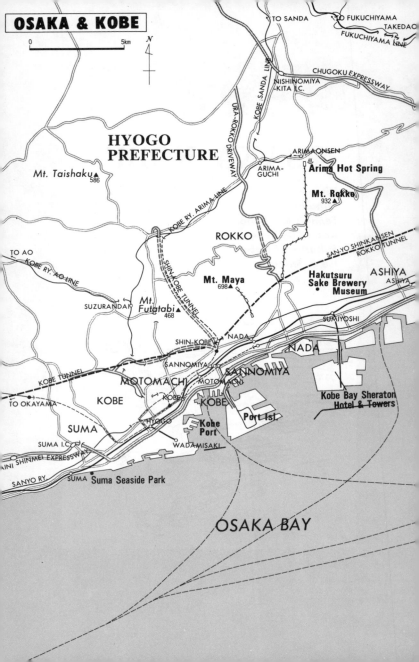

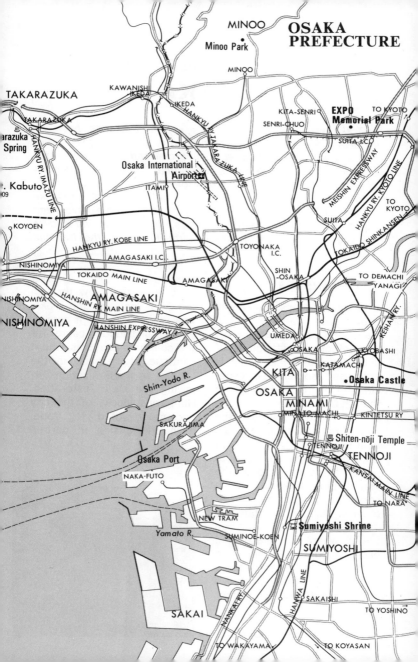

大 阪

OSAKA

Osaka was once the nation's capital and has been an important and successful trading center for centuries. Today, it is Japan's second largest commercial and industrial center and also takes pride in its traditional stage arts such as 'bunraku' and 'jōruri'. One point of interest in Osaka is its network of rivers and canals. These waterways helped Osaka prosper as a commercial city and although some have been lost to development in recent years, those remaining add to the character of this bustling central city of the Hanshin (Osaka - Kobe) Industrial zone.

HISTORY

In ancient times, Osaka was known as *Naniwa* (rapid waves), presumably on account of the difficulties of anchorage, and this name is still used sometimes, especially in poetry and songs. In the 4th C and again during the 6th and 7th centuries, the emperors had their palaces built here. But it was not until *Hideyoshi Toyotomi* rose to power as feudal lord in the 16th C that Osaka became a commercial city of consequence. As well as building Japan's grandest castle on the hill where the palaces had once stood, *Hideyoshi* also persuaded the merchants of neighboring towns to move into Osaka and carry on their business there. Osaka prospered and grew through the 265 years of the *Tokugawa* regime, when it operated as a distribution center for the country's products, and it continued to expand in the century of modernization following the Meiji restoration. Numerous blocks of the city became devoted to trade, each specializing in certain

Osaka Castle

types of goods. This association of different areas with certain products still remains, largely unchanged, today.

Osaka City

ACCESS

Tokyo (Haneda) to Osaka (Itami) by air: 1 hr. **Tokyo** to **Shin Osaka** by Tōkaidō Shikansen(Nozomi): 2 hr. 30min. **Tokyo** to **Osaka** by express sleeper on the JR Tōkaidō Line: 8 hr. 15 min; by JR Highway bus: 8 hr. 20 min. **Kyoto** to **Osaka** by JR Tōkaidō Line: 30 min, **Kyoto** to **Osaka (Namba)** by Kintetsu Railway: 1 hr. **Nara** to **Tennōji** by JR Kansai Line: 35 min. **Kobe (Sannomiya)** to **Osaka** by JR Tōkaidō Line: 20 min.

LOCAL TRANSPORTATION

The major stations which JR, private railways, subways and buses run from are Umeda in **Kita**, Namba in **Minami**, and Tennōji. JR operates a loop line (Osaka Kanjō line) with trains at frequent intervals in both directions. Osaka has a network of seven subway lines, which conveniently intersect with JR lines and other public transport. Taxis or rental cars are preferable to buses, since the bus system is rather complicated.

TOUR HINTS

Apart from a very hot summer, the weather in Osaka is pleasantly mild, with little rain. Accommodation is plentiful, with a wide range of hotels and traditional lodgings. Osaka is primarily a business city with an intense commercial atmosphere. There are, however, attractions that are unique to Osaka and places of interest which give the city an atmosphere totally different from the other major cities. The contrasts in Osaka can be seen by walking around both the modern *Kita* district around Osaka Station and the older *Minami* district around Namba. Osaka also has a well-deserved reputation for excellent dining. Kyoto and Nara can be reached in a short time from Osaka and could be considered as destinations after a day's sightseeing in Osaka.

127

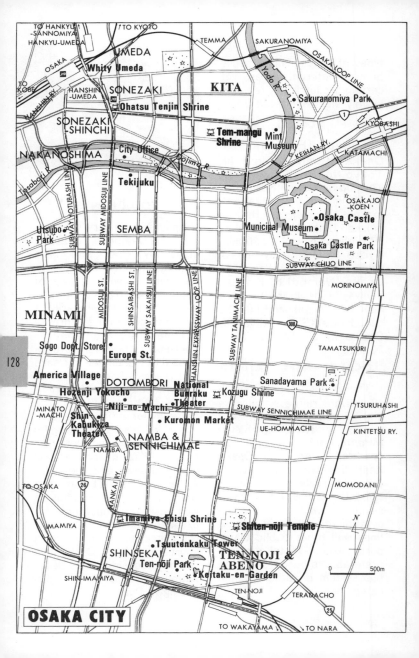

TO HANKYU-SANNOMIYA
HANKYU-UMEDA

TO KYOTO

TEMMA

SAKURANOMIYA

OSAKA LOOP LINE

UMEDA

Whity Umeda

OSAKA

TO KOBE

HANSHIN RY.

HANSHIN-UMEDA

SONEZAKI

KITA

Yodo R.

● Sakuranomiya Park

SONEZAKI-SHINCHI

☖ **Ohatsu Tenjin Shrine**

KYOBASHI

☖ **Tem-mangū Shrine**

Mint Museum

KEIHAN RY.

KATAMACHI

NAKANOSHIMA

City Office

Dojima R.

● **Tekijuku**

Osabori R.

SUBWAY YOTSUBASHI LINE

SUBWAY MIDOSUJI LINE

SEMBA

OSAKAJO-KOEN

Utsubo Park

Municipal Museum ●

● **Osaka Castle**

Osaka Castle Park

SUBWAY CHUO LINE

MORINOMIYA

MIDOSUJI ST.

SHINSAIBASHI ST.

SUBWAY SAKAISUJI LINE

SUBWAY TANIMACHI LINE

HANSHIN EXPRESSWAY LOOP LINE

308

MINAMI

TAMATSUKURI

Sogo Dept. Store ●

● **Europe St.**

● **America Village**

DOTOMBORI

National Bunraku Theater

☖ Kozugu Shrine

● Sanadayama Park

TSURUHASHI

Hōzenji Yokocho

● Niji-no-machi

SUBWAY SENNICHIMAE LINE

UE-HOMMACHI

KINTETSU RY.

MINATO-MACHI

Shin-Kabukiza Theater

● Kuromon Market

NAMBA & SENNICHIMAE

NAMBA

NANKAI RY.

TO OSAKA

26

MOMODANI

IMAMIYA

☖ **Imamiya-Ebisu Shrine**

☖ **Shiten-nōji Temple**

N

● Tsuutenkaku Tower

SHINSEKAI

Ten-nōji Park

TEN-NŌJI & ABENO

0   500m

SHIN-IMAMIYA

● Keitaku-en Garden

TEN-NŌJI

TERADACHO

25

OSAKA CITY

TO WAKAYAMA

TO NARA

128

WHAT TO SEE

KITA

The area around Osaka station along the Dōjima River, is generally called *Kita* by Osaka residents. **Osaka Castle**, the symbol of the city's long history, overlooks this district, which thrives as Osaka's business and entertainment center.

● *OSAKA CASTLE* Once the mightiest fortress in Japan, the castle was originally built in 1586 by the military ruler *Hideyoshi Toyotomi*. The *Toyotomi* family were annihilated when the castle was captured by *Tokugawa*, after fierce battles in 1615. The castle took 3 years to build and is noted for the immense granite stones — the largest 14.5m. long and 5.9m. long and 5.9m. high — used for the foundations and walls. Most of the castle was destroyed long ago and the present **Five-story Donjon** (eight stories inside) is a concrete reconstruction built in 1931, which reproduces the building's exterior. It towers 42m. high and commands an extensive view of the city. Elevators carry visitors to the top floor. Part of the donjon houses a museum containing many items of historical interest associated with the *Toyotomi* family and the development of the city. At night the donjon is illuminated and stands out in brilliant relief. Near Ōte - mae bus stop.

● *SEMBA* This area plays an important role in Osaka's commerce and includes **Kitahama**, the stockbroking district, **Doshōmachi**, with its many pharmaceutical businesses and **Dobuike**, center of the clothing and textile trade. *Hideyoshi Toyotomi* had canals built to allow commercial craft access to the area, but these have since been reclaimed for commercial building. Although Semba is a bustling, modern business area, some traces of its past still remain in its old stores and restaurants. Yodoyabashi subway station.

● *TEKIJUKU* *Kōan Ogata* (1810—1863), a doctor and

129

Nakanoshima

scholar, opened a school called *Tekijuku* in the 19th C. He taught western subjects and several of his students became prominent successes in various fields. The school building, which resembles a traditional merchant's house, has been preserved and is open to the public. 7 min. walk from Yodoyabashi subway station.

● *NAKANOSHIMA* Located on a small island between the Dōjima and Tosabori rivers, Nakanoshima is a civic center containing many prefectural and municipal government buildings. Many western style buildings built in the late 19th and early 20th centuries still stand on its streets. 2 min. walk from Yodoyabashi subway station.

● *TEM-MANGU SHRINE* Temmangū was founded in 949 in memory of *Michizane Sugawara,* a great literary scholar of the 9th C, and it is to this shrine that large numbers of students come to pray for help in passing their examinations. The *Tenjin Matsuri* festival is held here on July 24 and 25. 3 min. walk from Minamimorimachi subway station.

● *UMEDA* The area centered around Osaka (Umeda) Station is a bustling business and entertainment district with numerous department stores, office buildings, shops, restaurants and theaters crowding its streets.

● *WHITY UMEDA* Underneath Osaka Station and its vicinity, this vast arcade covers 17,000 sq.m. and contains numerous souvenir shops, fruit and vegetable markets, teahouses and restaurants. Its passages connect with JR and private railway stations as well as major buildings and department stores.

Many souvenir stores are located near the entrance

TENJIN MATSURI

This is one of Japan's three biggest festivals and a very lively one. Its numerous events include *Rikutogyo*, when *mikoshi* (portable shrines) are paraded through the city and then taken aboard ships for the nighttime *Funatogyo* parade, with about 80 ships sailling up the Dōjima River. The festival takes place on July 24 and 25 every year.

American Village

of Hankyū Department store.

● **SONEZAKI** This arcade runs from *Umeda Kagetsu* Theater towards Ohatsu Tenjin Shrine and is the center of a lively entertainment district. Bars, cabarets, pubs and restaurants vie for custom on its backstreets and even surround the shrine itself. Near Higashi Umeda subway station

● **OHATSU TENJIN SHRINE** Hidden away in the Sonezaki district, this shrine is the setting of the famous story, *Sonezaki Shinjū* (Lover's Suicide at Sonezaki), a tale based on the tragic romance of *Ohatsu,* a prostitute, and her lover. The story was later dramatized by *Monzaemon Chikamatsu* (1653-1724), the most popular playwright of the Edo era. As a consequence, the shrine, originally called *Tsuyunoten Shrine,* became popularly known as Ohatsu Tenjin. 8 min. walk from JR Osaka Station.

MINAMI

Osaka's *Minami* (South) district provides striking contrasts to the *Kita* district. Where as *Kita* is intensely commercial, with modern buildings and shopping areas, the older *Minami* district still retains the atmosphere of earlier days, with lively streets full of shops and restaurants.

● **SHINSAIBASHI-SUJI & MIDŌ-SUJI** Shinsaibashi-suji runs parallel to Midōsuji and its southern end is a popular shopping area, filled with department stores and specialty shops. Midōsuji, a wide boulevard lined with ginkgo trees, is the city's main thoroughfare, running through central Osaka from Umeda in the north to Namba in the south. Near Shinsaibashi subway station.

● **AMERICAN VILLAGE** Visitors may be amused by this lively 'Village', situated west of Midōsuji. Here, watched over by a statue of the Goddess of Liberty and a huge fresco entitled 'Peace on Earth', crowds of young people shop for American-style new and second-hand clothes, accessories and imported records.

●*EUROPE STREET* Situated in the block opposite the one containing the American Village, across Midōsuji, this street is lined with boutiques and specialty shops selling all kinds of top-brand imported European clothing and other goods. Near Shinsaibashi subway station.

●*DŌTOMBORI* Dōtombori Canal, constructed by *Dōton Yasui* in the l7th C runs through this area, Minami's popular entertainment quarter. Dōtombori is particularly attractive at night, when multi - colored neon signs on cabarets and nightclubs in Soemon-chō and those on restaurants on Dōtombori Street are reflected on the surface of the canal. 5 min. walk from Namba subway sta-

tion.

●*HŌZENJI YOKOCHŌ* Not far from the bustling Sennichi-mae is Hōzenji Temple, noted for its moss-covered *Mizukake Fudō* statues, which stand in a bower, adorned with paper lanterns. The temple is in a narrow, stone-paved alley, crowded with tiny restaurants and bars. Hōzenji alley became well-known after appearing in a novel by *Sakunosuké Oda. A monument to this Osaka novelist stands in the alley.

●*SEN-NICHI-MAE & NAMBA* Sen-nichi-mae Street has been an entertainment quarter since the late Meiji era, when slapstick and comic plays were staged. Now the area abounds in cinemas, *pachinko* parlors, variety theaters, cabarets and nightclubs. Namba is at the southern end of Midōsuji Street, within walking distance of Sen-nichi-mae. It is a major junction for suburban railways and features underground arcades, department stores and wholesalers catering to the restaurant trade. Near Namba subway station.

●*NIJI-NO-MACHI* This 800 m. long arcade beneath Sen-nichi-maé Street has exits leading to the Ebisubashi, Sen-nichi-maé and Nippom-bashi areas.

Mizukake Fudō Statue

At the exits are interesting places to sit and take a break — a Square of Light, Square of Water and Square of Green.

● **NAMBA CITY** In the Namba Station building of the Nankai Dentetsu Line is this 'City of the 21st century', a modern shopping complex with clothing, audio-visual and sports stores, theaters, restaurants and event spaces. It consists of two 3-storied buildings and the station is on the 2nd floor of the main building.

● **NATIONAL BUNRAKU THEATER** Osaka's citizens are justly proud of their contribution to the world's performing arts— *Bunraku* puppet theater. Performances can be seen in this well-known theater, the national headquarters of the art. 2 min. walk from Nippombashi subway station.

● *SHIN-KABUKIZA THEATER* This Momoyama-era style building opened in 1958 to stage *kabuki* performances. These days, modern drama prevails at the theater and *kabuki* plays are performed only occasionally. Near Namba Station of the Nankai Railway.

● *KUROMON MARKET* An interesting place to look around in, this food market does a large trade with *sushi*

NANIWA HAPPYAKUYA-BASHI (NANIWA'S 808 BRIDGES)

With its many rivers, Osaka used to be known as 'the city on water' and accordingly had numerous bridges, earning it the title of '*Naniwa Happyakuya-bashi*'. At the end of the 18th C, before many of the rivers were reclaimed, there were still over 150 bridges. Hommachi-bashi, built in 1913, is the oldest existing bridge but many of the old bridges, like Shin-saibashi, now remain only as placenames in the city.

---

bars and restaurants, selling fresh fish. It is crowded with restauranteurs in the early morning and housewives in the afternoon. 2 min. walk from Nippombashi subway station.

TEN-NOJI & ABENO

These popular districts in the southern end of the city area are crowded with restaurants and theaters and have well-known, historically important temples and shrines.

● **SHITEN-NOJI TEMPLE** Popularly called Ten-nōji, the temple was founded in 593 by Prince *Shōtoku* and its stone *torii* gate, the oldest in Japan, has stood since 1294.

The temple predates even Hōryūji Temple in Nara, which has a similar layout, and its buildings represent Japan's oldest style of temple construction, now known as the *Shiten-nōji* style. Unfortunately, none of the original buildings remain and the Main Hall, Kondō, Kōdō, the Five-Storied Pagoda and other buildings are all post-war reconstructions. 5 min. walk south of Shitennōji-mae subway station.

● **TEN-NŌJI PARK** This large western-style public park contains a zoo, botanical gardens, greenhouses, Keitaku-en Garden and cultural facilities including the municipal library and art gallery. It also has an old gateway, which once belonged to the house of a feudal clan. Near Ten-nōji Station on the Nankai Electric Railway.

● **KEITAKU-EN GARDEN** Situated beside the Municipal Art Gallery, this very pretty garden is an excellent example of the Japanese pond-centered strolling garden. Over 8,000sq.m. in area, it once formed part of the residence of a wealthy family and was donated to the city in 1926.

● **SHINSEKAI** Shinsekai, on the western side of Ten-nōji Park, has long been one of Osaka's more infamous entertainment areas. All tastes are catered for here and cinemas, strip joints, games parlors, *shōgi* clubs, *pachinko* parlors and restaurants are tightly packed in a small block around Jan-jan-yokochō. Near Ebisu-chō subway station.

● **TSŪTENKAKU TOWER** Originally built in 1912, the tower was temporarily pulled down during the war and re-erected in 1956. This landmark stands about 103 m. high and has an observation platform at 91 m. for viewing the city.

● **IMAMIYA EBISU SHRINE** Osaka folk call this shrine *Ebessan*, since *Ebisu*, the God of Wealth, is worshipped here. *Ebisu* was at first wor-

Shinsekai

shipped by fishermen and then the fish merchants from the market near Shiten-nōji Temple and now by everyone interested in prosperity. The shrine sanctuary is always quiet and peaceful except on *Tōka Ebisu* on January 10th, when people gather to pray for a prosperous year. Near Imamiya Ebisu Station on the Nankai Electric Railway.

● *SUMIYOSHI SHRINE*
Believed to have been founded by Empress *Jingū* in 202, this shrine is dedicated to four deities including guardians of travelers. The present main buildings are reconstructions from 1808, all National Treasures, built in the *Sumiyoshi-zukuri* style with roofs covered with multiple layers of thin wood strips. The grounds contain an arched stone bridge with vermilion railings, donated by *Hideyoshi Toyotomi*, and the approach is lined with over 700 stone lanterns, donated by seamen, shipowners and merchants from around Japan. East of Sumiyoshi Taisha Station on the Nankai Electric Railway.

● *SUMIYOSHI PARK* West of Sumiyoshi Shrine is this popular park, noted for its huge pine and camphor trees. The pines once grew on the beach

EXPO Memorial Park

but are now separated from it by reclaimed land.

● *EXPO MEMORIAL PARK* This large recreational and cultural center was constructed on the former site of the 1970 World Exposition. The park's facilities include the Expo Commemoration Hall, the National Museum of Ethnology, the Japan Folk Crafts Museum and Expo Land, an amusement park. 5 min. by monorail from Senri-Chūō subway station.

135

WHERE TO EAT

Osaka is regarded as a gourmet's paradise and the city abounds in cheap, friendly restaurants serving great food. Minami is the best district for dining and in the Dōtombori area you'll find **Kuidaore**, a popular building with 8 floors of pubs, cafes and restaurants. The taste of

Shinsaibashi-suji

true Osaka cooking can be savored at **Matsubaya** with the likes of *kitsune udon* (noodles and fried tōfu). **Honfuku-zushi** serves traditional *Osaka sushi,* which is pressed into squares and topped with marinated fish. **Shōben Tango-tei** is another noted restaurant and the favorite of the late novelist *Sakunosuke Oda*. **Meijiken** serves Japanese Western dishes like omelette rice. A top-class Western restaurant is **Alaska**, in Nakanoshima. **Mimiu** is a traditional noodle shop serving Osaka's specialty, *Udon-suki*. With this dish, you are served fish, vegetables and thick noodles, which you boil by yourself in a pot of lightly seasoned soup. Shops selling *Udon-suki* can be found easily around railway stations.

WHAT TO BUY

Department stores such as **Hankyū, Hanshin** and **Daimaru** around Osaka Station and stores in the Shinsaibashi area provide interesting shopping, especially for clothes. In the food line, two traditional souvenirs are *awaokoshi*, a dry sweet made from foxtail plant millet, found at **Tsu-no-sei** in Dōtombori and *tsurigane manjū*, a bell-shaped dumpling sold at **Sōhonke Tsuriganeya**.

NIGHTLIFE

Osaka has all the nightclubs, cabarets, and bars found in any large Japanese city. Four suggestions are: **West Coast** an American style wine house near Osaka Station, the English pub, **Duke of Wellington**, the palatial disco **Samba Club** and the **Yoshida Bar**, which, since opening in 1931, has been a good place for a quiet drink.

Hanshin Department Store

神 戸

KOBE

Kobe extends for nearly 35km. from east to west over a scenic belt of land nestled between the Rokkō mountain range and Osaka Bay. As well as being an industrial and commercial city, it is also one of Japan's largest ports, handling over 14,000 vessels a year. As an international seaport, Kobe has attracted a large foreign population and enjoys a cosmopolitan atmosphere. The appearance of the city — modern shopping streets, western architecture preserved from the Meiji era and a picturesque natural setting — also contributes to Kobe's unique atmosphere.

HISTORY

Kobe has played an important role in sea transportation since ancient times and, as early as the 4th C, it was a gateway through which Chinese and Korean culture filtered into Japan. In the 12th C *Taira-no-Kiyomori,* the military ruler, carried out a huge harbor construction plan in an attempt to develop foreign trade, and temporarily moved the capital here from Kyoto. Its reign as capital lasted only six months but its port, Hyōgo, continued to prosper. In 1867, the port of Kobe, a short distance northeast of Hyōgo, was opened for foreign trade. Since then Kobe has developed dramatically as a city and an international and domestic port.

ACCESS

Tokyo to Shin-Kobe by Tōkaidō Shinkansen: 3hr. 10min. Osaka to Sannomiya by JR Express: 20min. Umeda to Hankyū Sannomiya by Hankyū Line Limited Express: 30min. Umeda to Hanshin Sannomiya by Hanshin Line Limited Express: 30min. Kyoto to Sannomiya by JR Express: 50min. Osaka International Airport to Sannomiya by bus: 40min.

LOCAL TRANSPORTATION

The Shinkansen stops at Shin-Kobe Station. From there to Sannomiya, the city center, it is 2min. by subway or 5min. by taxi. JR, Hanshin and Hankyū Railway lines run parallel from east to west across the city. There is an extensive bus network but most attractions are within easy walking distance from Sannomiya and Motomachi, the major central stations. Cruising taxis are available.

TOUR HINTS

Kobe enjoys a temperate climate but is quite wet in June and cold in winter. There are some hotels in the downtown area, but pleasant and convenient alternatives might be the inns near Arima or Takerazuka hot-springs resorts.

Day 1 Sannomiya — Foreigners' Residences in Kitano — Sōrakuen Garden — Kanteibyō Temple—Motomachi—Kobe Port—Sannomiya.

Day 2 Arima Spa—Mt. Rokkō —Nada-Gogō Sake Brewery.

WHAT TO SEE

KOBE CITY

The old foreign residential area, **Sōrakuen Garden**, the parks, the Chinatown of **Nankin-machi** and the port itself are interesting places to visit. Sannomiya and **Motomachi** offer good shopping and dining.

● *SANNOMIYA* This is Kobe's most popular central shopping district. On the south side of the JR station are numerous department stores and busy streets include **Flower Road** and **Sannomiya Center-gai**, while underground is fashionable **Sanchika Town**.

● *SANCHIKA TOWN* Flower Road runs through this area which extends southwards to the port. The arcade, decorated with statues and art works, contains shops, restaurants, information center, 'Information Kobe'.

● *SANNOMIYA CENTER-GAI* This busy shopping street southwest of Sannomiya Station leads to Motomachi, parallel to JR's elevated railway tracks.

The modern tall buildings along the covered arcade, such as **Sun Plaza, Center Plaza** and **Center Plaza-West Wing,** contain a myriad of fashion boutiques, restaurants and cafes.

● *TOR ROAD* Leading north from **Daimaru** department store to the foreign residential area of Kitano, the road lends this part of the city a somewhat exotic flavor, It is lined with stylish restaurants, antique shops and boutiques displaying a wide range of imported goods. 5min. walk west of Sannomiya Station.

●**MOTOMACHI** The highlight here is the covered arcade extending between Motomachi and Sannomiya Stations. There are many long-established stores here, including antique shops, variety stores, secondhand book-stores and also restaurants and tea-houses. Stores are often filled with visiting sailors looking for good bargains. Motomachi Station on JR and Hanshin Lines.

●**KŌKASHITA SHŌTEN-GAI** Stretching along under JR's tracks between Sannomiya and Kobe via Motomachi, this is a different type of shopping arcade with a narrow, low-roofed promenade full of tiny shops.

● **NANKIN MACHI** In the first block along Motomachi Street, the lanterns and Chinese style two-storied iron gate will tell you that you are in Kobe's small Chinatown.

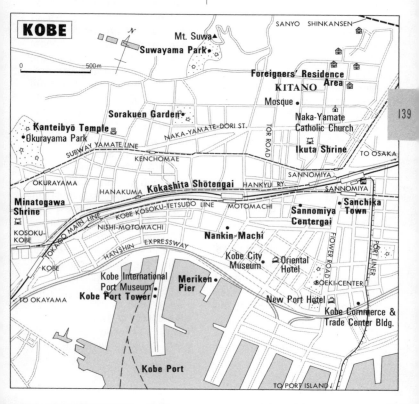

139

Here you can find Chinese restaurants and shops selling food, clothes and curios. In the center of the town is China Plaza, a popular spot for a breather for both visitors and residents. Motomachi 1-chōme bus stop.

● **MINATOGAWA SHRINE**
Popularly known as *Nankōsan*, this shrine is dedicated to *Masashige Kusunoki*, a valiant warrior general in medieval times. Camphor trees grow in the shrine grounds, where his grave can be found. Worth seeing here is the great dragon decorating the ceiling of the sanctuary and the woodblock prints by the renowned artist, *Shikō Munakata.* 3min. walk north of JR Kobe Station.

● **KITANO** It was here that many foreigners lived during the Taishō and Meiji eras. Dotted about the hillside overlooking the port are old houses, churches and Chinese temples. 15min. walk from either Sannomiya or Shin-Kobe Station.

● **FOREIGNERS' RESIDENCES**
Extremely popular with Japanese visitors, some of the old western-style houses here are well-preserved and several are open to the public. Here you can find houses with red chimneys, white weather

vanes, and other typically western architecture. Bay windows and in their rows they make a lovely sight against the green backdrop of the mountains. *Kazamidori-no-Yakata* is the only brick house in the Kitano area and other popular houses are the *Uroko-no-Yakata* and *white house*. Also here is the **Persian Gallery** displaying Persian arts and antiques.

● **SŌRAKUEN GARDEN** This is a typical Japanese landscape garden with a small grove of 200-year old cycads and camphor trees. Azaleas bloom here in the spring and the garden also contains western-style buildings from the Meiji era, including a brick stable and the Hussam Residence, former home of a foreign merchant. 10min. walk north of Motomachi Station.

● **SUWAYAMA PARK** This well-wooded hill park is a pleasant place for a stroll. The viewpoint known as **Venus Bridge** has traditionally been a favorite spot for tourists and local lovers to admire the romantic sight of the city at night. 10min. by bus from Sannomiya Station then a 3min. walk.

● **KANTEIBYŌ TEMPLE** This temple, revered by Kobe's many Chinese residents, was built to worship Kan'u a Chinese warrior . Its roof and pillars decorated in bright, rich colors and the stone lions in the grounds make it clearly different from a Japanese temple. 3min. walk from Shimo-Yamate 8-chōme bus stop.

● *IKUTA SHRINE* The shrine lies in the heart of the busy commercial area near Sannomiya Station and is dedicated to *Wakahirume-no-Mikoto*, a mythological female deity and guardian of Kobe's citizens. As such it attracts large numbers of visitors. Its vermilion buildings, recently reconstructed, are very attractive. 7min. walk northwest of Sannomiya Station.

● *KOBE PORT* Naturally this is Kobe's major feature and a constant hive of activity with some 14,000 passenger and cargo liners visiting annually. It has been a port since the 3rd C and today has more than a dozen piers. The best known of these are the Naka (Central), Maya and Meriken piers. Naka pier is also the terminal for ferries to and from Shikoku and Kyūshū. A good way to view the port is to take the 50min. Port Cruise, which leaves from the quay in front of the Port Tower.

● *MERIKEN PIER* Constructed in 1868, the name of this 200m. pier, east of Naka Pier, derives from the fact that the American Consulate once stood nearby. Today, the pier is used by harbor boats and for launchings. It once featured in an old Japanese popular song and hence is a place of some nostalgia for Japanese visitors. 5min. walk from Naka-tottei bus stop.

● *PORT TOWER* This stands 108m. high on Naka Pier and resembles a *tsuzumi* (Japanese hend-drum). It features a revolving observation platform commanding a panoramic view. The 3rd and 4th floors of the central passenger departure building house a museum complete with audio-visual aids to explain the activities of the port. Naka Pier also has a passenger departure building with a bridge extending to the 3rd floor of the Port Tower. 5min. walk south of Sakae-chō

141

Kobe Port

Port Island

3-chōme bus stop.

● **PORT ISLAND** This man-made island was the site of the exposition 'Portopia 81', which had as its main theme a 'Cultural community on the Various cultural facilities have been built here with the aim of making the island a 'cultural community on the sea'. They include parks, hotels, apartment buildings, sports centers, a science museum and the **International Conference Center.** Near Minami-kōen Station is **Portopia Land,** an amusement park featuring the great '**Giant Wheel**'. The automatic **Portliner** train circles the island, making 6 stops in front of major buildings and facilities. 17min. by Portliner from Sannomiya Station to Minami-kōen on the south side of the island.

● **KOBE CITY MUSEUM** A museum of Kobe's archaeology, history and folklore, it is connected with the Kobe City Museum of *Namban* Art, which exhibits a fine collection of Japanese paintings and art works produced in the 16th and 17th centuries, which show degrees of European influence. 8min. walk from Sannomiya Station.

SUBURBS OF KOBE

Several attractions in Kobe's outskirts will add interest to a visit here. They include the *sake* brewers town of **Nada,** Mt. Rokkō and the resorts of **Arima** and **Takarazuka.**

● **HAKUTSURU SAKE BREWERY MUSEUM** *Nada Gogō* is an area with old and modern *sake* breweries. With an abundance of natural spring water, excellent rice and skilled workers, it is hardly surprising that the region produces some of Japan's finest sake. The museum in the Hakutsuru Brewery grounds exhibits old tools and utensils and illustrates the *sake*-brewing process by using life-size models. 5min. walk from Sumiyoshi Station on the Hanshin Electric Railway.

● **MT. ROKKŌ** The Rokkō mountain chain bordering Kobe city runs for 54km. and the highest peak is 932m. The mountain has numerous

142

facilites including an observatory, an amusement park, golf links, artificial ski slope and hotels. The mountain is the best site to enjoy the wonderful night view of the city and Osaka Bay. 15min. by bus from Hankyū Rokkō Station to Rokkō Cable Car Station, 10min. to the summit. The Rokkō - Arima Ropeway links the summit with Arima Spa.

● **MT. MAYA** This is the second highest peak in the Rokkō Range at 698m. and it also offers superb views and recreational facilities. Near the summit is Tenjōji Temple, dedicated to *Maya Bunin*, mother of Gautama Buddha, after whom the mountain was named. 20min. by bus from JR Sannomiya Station to Maya Cable Car bus stop. By cable car to Maya Station is 5min. and then it is 5min. by ropeway to the summit.

● **ARIMA SPA** This secluded hot-spring resort lies in a valley on the northern base of Mt. Rokkō and is known as one of the oldest spas in the country. There are around 30 Japanese inns here, each with its own hot-spring baths and the town also features tennis courts and archery halls. The spa is a cool retreat in cherry blossom and maple-viewing seasons. 40min. by bus from Sannomiya Station; or 12min. by cable car from the summit of Mt. Rokkō.

● **SUMA** Here you will find white sandy beachs lined with pine trees, the only bathing beaches on the coast between Kobe and Osaka. Also in the **Suma Beach Park** is the Suma Aquarium. A little further west on the mountainside is **Suma-ura Park**, from where a ropeway leads to Mt. Hachibuse. 12min. by JR train from Sannomiya Station.

● *TAKARAZUKA* Takarazuka is a spa resort in the suburban zone between Osaka and Kobe. A big attraction here is Family Land, comprising a zoo, botanical gardens, hot-spring baths, science museum and amusement facilities. The other main attraction is **Takarazuka Grand Theater** which presents a variety of colorful revues and musicals by the noted all-female Takarazuka Revue troupe, who

143

Arima Spa

Kobe Beef

train at the school attached to the theater. From Umeda, 35min. by express train on the Hankyū Takarazuka Line.

WHERE TO EAT

As a port, Kobe has naturally assimilated foreign culture and along with it, foreign cuisine. As well as bread and confectionery, Kobe is renowned for its high-quality beef, prepared in a variety of ways. **Rengatei** on Tor Road cooks beef with Japanese paper attached and **Aburi-niku-kōbō Wakkoku** in Kitano grills steak from only the black cattle raised in Tajima. Kitano has many international restaurants such as the French **Bistro de Lyon**, the **Swiss Chalet** and the Spanish **El Pancho Kitano** which features flamenco dancing. For Chinese food, Nankin Machi has lots to offer. Regular Cantonese dishes can be tried at **Minsei Kanton Ryōriten**.

WHAT TO BUY

Sannomiya is packed with shops and department stores like **Printemps**, **Sogo** and **Hankyū** which offer the best in Japanese and imported clothing. The underground **Sanchika Town** sells a variety of quality goods for everyday use. **Marukiya** is an interesting antique shop on Tor Road. For nicely designed stationery, try **One Way**. The Motomachi area, in contrast to Sannomiya, is an older shopping area and its shops reflect something of Kobe's past.

NIGHTLIFE

A great place to take in Kobe's splendid night views over a meal and drinks is the restaurant **Plein d'Etoiles** on the 31st floor of the Portopia Hotel. **Nunobiki** in the New port Hotel is a classy bar with a relaxing atmosphere. You can also sample a little of the old world by hearing chansons sung live at **Etoi** or having a few beers in the English interior of the **Kings Arms**, or simply dance the night away at the popular disco **VINC**.

伊勢・志摩
ISE & SHIMA

Ise and Shima are among the longest settled parts of the country and Ise Jingū Shrine is the country's most important Shintō shrine, to which people from all over Japan have long made pilgrimage. Shima Peninsula is also known for its cultured pearls, its pretty coastal scenery and lush farmland. The area can easily be included in visits to the Kyoto - Osaka region and is reached in a short time on the Kintetsu Line from Osaka or Nagoya. To Ise, Kintetsu Line express trains take Ihr. 46min. from Osaka and around 2hrs. from Kyoto.

WHAT TO SEE

● *ISE - SHIMA NATIONAL PARK*
The park covers a large area in the southern extremity of Mie Prefecture with numerous resort towns scattered around its pretty inlets on the Rias coastline.

● *ISE JINGŪ SHRINE* The central feature of the National Park is the grand shrines in Ise city, the most revered of all Japanese shrines, still visited by the imperial family. There are two shrine complexes, *Naikū* (Inner Shrine) in Ise city and *Gekū* (Outer Shrine) situated 6km away outside the city. Buses run between the two.

Naikū is somewhat more important as it honors and is considered the abode of *Amaterasu*, the sun goddess

and the highest deity in the Shintō pantheon. *Gekū* is dedicated to *Toyouke - Ōmikami*, the goddess of agriculture.

In both shrines, all buildings are constructed in the ancient style used before the introduction of Chinese architecture. They have a beautiful simplicity and plainness—the roofs are thatched and the buildings are constructed of unpainted cypress, assembled entirely without nails. An

145

Ise Jingū Shrine

interesting feature of the shrines is that they are regularly torn down and replaced with a new set of identical buildings. 10min. walk from Ise-shi Station to Gekū.

● **FUTAMIGAURA** In a small bay here are a celebrated pair of rocks known as *Meoto - iwa* (Husband and Wife Rocks) standing in the sea close to the beach. The bay developed as a place for purification before proceeding to Ise Jingū Shrine and consequently numerous hotels and inns have sprung up here. 5min. walk from Futami bus stop.

● **TOBA & PEARL ISLAND** From Toba bay a 50min. boat trip takes in pearl rafts, pearl diving by women divers and a visit to **Mikimoto Pearl Island**. The island is also connected to the main-land by a bridge. The **Pearl Museum** here displays various materials related to pearl cultivation and to the life of *Kōkichi Mikimoto* (1858 — 1954), who lived on the island and in 1893 became the first person to successfully produce a cultured pearl. 20min. from Ise-shi Station.

TOBA AQUARIUM This very interesting aquarium keeps a variety of marine life including dugongs, sea otters, dolphins, shellfish and the world's smallest whale, neomeris phocaenoide, the mammal which led to the myth of the mermaid. 7min. walk south of Toba Station.

KASHIKOJIMA Kashikojima Island and Ago Bay are central attractions in Ise - Shima National Park, with their quiet, wooded inlets and pretty seascapes. The **National Pearl Research Institute** is located on the island and Ago Bay and neighboring bays are covered with rafts used for raising pearl oysters. These can be seen from the many sightseeing boats which operate around the bays. About 40min. from Toba by the Kintetsu Line.

SHOPPING & DINING

Ise is noted for confectionery called *Shōgatō*, and *Akafuku*, a rice cake containing bean jam. Toba is the home of pearls and those produced on **Mikimoto pearl Island** are of excellent quality.

Kashikojima Island

TRAVEL HINTS

❖

GENERAL INFORMATION

ENTERING THE COUNTRY

TRAVEL DOCUMENTS

You'll need a passport of course. When you arrive at immigration, present the passport and the entry card you filled out on the plane or boat you arrived on. Make sure you don't lose your copy until you leave the country.

VISAS

Unless you have an exemption, a valid passport containing a visa from a Japanese Embassy or Consulate is required for entry into Japan.

Tourist Visa: If you visit Japan to sightsee, visit relatives, participate in meetings, short study courses, or sports, or similar activities not involving remuneration, you can apply for a tourist visa. The term you can stay in Japan depends upon your nationality and purpose.

Documents Required to Apply For a Tourist Visa: The applicant must usually submit to a Japanese Embassy or Consulate the following: 1) A valid passport; 2) Two copies of the completed visa application forms (a passport-sized photograph must be affixed in most cases); 3) An air or sea passage ticket to and from Japan or evidence of possession thereof.

INOCULATION

No vaccinations are required to enter Japan from any country except for coming via infected areas.

ANIMAL AND PLANT QUARANTINE

Any animals and plants to be imported are subject to quarantine inspection upon arrival at Japanese ports.

CUSTOMS

Customs declaration: An oral declaration of one's belongings will suffice except when: 1) arriving by ship; 2) having unaccompanied baggage arriving on a later flight; or 3) having articles in excess of the duty free allowance (see next page). In these cases one must make a written declaration to the customs officer. (A written declaration must be made at the time and place of entry. Otherwise a claim for duty free import of unaccompanied baggage will not be accepted.)

Free Import: Personal effects and professional equipment can be brought into Japan duty free as long as their contents and quantities are deemed reasonable by the customs officer. The articles listed below can also be imported duty free within the quantities indicated.

1) 400 cigarettes or 500 grams of tobacco or 100 cigars (no allowance for persons aged 19 years or younger.)

2) 3 bottles (760c.c. each) of alcoholic beverages. (No allowance for persons aged 19 years or younger).

3) 2 oz. of perfume

4) Gifts and souvenirs whose total market price is less than ¥200,000 or its equivalent value.

Import and Export of Currency: Import of foreign currencies is unlimited; Japanese currency up to ¥5 million. Export of foreign currencies is unlimited; Japanese currency up to ¥5 million.

DEPARTING THE COUNTRY

Departure tax:
It's not exactly a tax but all departing passengers on international flights leaving from Narita Airport will be charged a Passenger Service Facility Charge of ¥2,000 (¥1,000 for children aged 2 to 12 years).Transit passengers continuing their travels by the same or first connecting flights on the same day are not taxed; nor are infants aged 2 years or younger; or state guests and other official guests. There is no charge at Osaka or at other international airports.

Free export: (Not for commercial purposes). Reasonable quantities of tobacco products, alcoholic beverages, perfume, gifts, and other articles.

Articles purchased tax-free in Japan must be shown to the Customs officer at the airport / port of departure from Japan.

LANGUAGE

The official language is Japanese. However, English is understood in most first class hotels and tourist oriented facilities.

TIME ZONES

All Japan is in the same time zone, 9 hours ahead of G.M.T.

Daylight saving time is not in effect here.

CURRENCY

The unit of Japanese currency is yen (indicated by ¥). Coin denominations are 1, 5, 10, 50, 100 and 500 yen. The most commonly used coins are ¥10, ¥50, ¥100, and ¥500. Bank notes (bills) are ¥1,000, ¥5,000, and ¥10,000.

Yen can be bought at foreign exchange banks and other authorized money changers (found in department stores, hotels, etc.) on showing your passport. Travelers checks can also be cashed into yen. It is advisable for the visitor to carry U.S. dollars or pound sterling travelers checks whenever possible.

TRAVELERS CHECKS

These can be used at 1st class hotels, department stores, duty free shops, and similar places. They cannot be used at regular shops and restaurants because those places are not authorized to convert currency, so you will need cash in yen.

CREDIT CARDS

The following credit cards are accepted at most hotels, department stores, restaurants, etc.: *American Express, Visa International, Carte Blanche, Diners Club, and Master Card.*

TIPPING

Tipping is not a common practice in Japan. To obviate the need for individual tipping, a 10 to 15 percent service charge will be added to your bill in some hotels and restaurants. But for the most part, no gratuity is required.

ELECTRICITY

The electric current for home use is uniformly 100 volts AC throughout Japan but there are two different frequencies in use — 50 in eastern Japan, which includes Tokyo, and 60 in western Japan, which includes Nagoya, Kyoto, and Osaka.

DRINKING WATER

Japan has abundant clean water in its mountain streams. The tap water is germ-free and can be drunk without precautions.

WEIGHTS AND MEASURES

l kilometer(km.)=0.621 miles;	l mile = 1.609km.
l meter (m.) = 1.094 yards;	l yard = 0.914 m.
l meter (m.) = 3.280 feet;	l foot = 0.305 m.
l centimeter (cm.) = 0.39 inch;	l inch = 2.54 cm.
l kilogram (kg) = 2.205 lbs;	l lb = 0.454 kg
l liter (ℓ) = 0.264 U.S. gal;	l U.S. gal. = 3.785 liters
l liter (ℓ) = 0.22 lmp. gal;	l lmp.gal. = 4.546 liters

POSTAL SERVICES

The simple way to mail your letters and packages is to get assistance from the front desk in your hotel. Postal rates within Japan are ¥62 up to 25 grams, and ¥72 up to 50 grams, if the envelope is between 9×14 cm and 12×23.5 cm. Mail that does not fit within the above measurements costs ¥120 up to 50 grams, and ¥175 up to 100 grams. Postcards cost ¥41.

Air Mail Rates

	Asia	Oceania, Near & Middle East, North & Central Americas	Europe, Africa, South America
Postcards	¥ 70	¥ 70	¥ 70
Aerograms	¥ 80	¥ 80	¥ 80
Letters:(Up to 10 grams)	¥ 80	¥100	¥120
(Each extra 10 grams)	¥ 60	¥ 70	¥100

151

TELEPHONE

PUBLIC TELEPHONE

Public telephones of various colors are found on almost every street corner in Japan. All of them accept ¥10 coins, but yellow and green (and recently some red ones) accept ¥100,

Telephone Charges from Tokyo to Kinki Region

Place	Area Code	Number of seconds per ¥100
Kyoto	075	90
Nara	0742	90
Osaka	06	90
Kobe	078	90

convenient for calling long distance. A local call costs ¥10 for 3 minutes and all unused coins will be returned, but no change is given for ¥100 coins. You can make direct inter-city calls from these phones. Green phones accept a magnetic pre-paid card, *Telephone Card*, available at local phone companies.

INTERNATIONAL CALLS

There are two ways to place international calls from Japan. One is to make direct (ISD=International Subscriber Dialing) calls from telephones which have been registered for ISD with KDD. Make sure that this service is available because it is not wide-spread in Japan. To call, dial 001, 0041 or 0061+country code+area code+desired number. Another is to place your call through the KDD operator. Simply dial 0051 and you'll get the KDD operator. If you're calling from a hotel, ask the desk to place a call.

International Telephone Charges (*Unit—Yen*) **As of May lst, 1993**

Area	Country Code	ISDCalls(Per 6 Second)			Station-to-Station Calls	Person-to-Person Calls	Each Additional Minute
		Standard Rate	Economy Rate	Discount Rate	Initial 3 Minutes		
U.S.A (Mainland)	1	34	27	20	1,700	2,900	440
United Kingdom	44	43	34	26	2,060	3,500	510
Australia	61	38	30	23	1,530	3,050	470
Korea	82	34	27	20	1,620	2,160	440
Hong Kong	852	36	29	22	1,620	2,160	460
Singapore	65	38	30	23	1,830	2,880	470

	0	8	19	23 24	
Mon.-Fri.					Standard Rate
Sat., Sun., National Holidays					Economy Rate (Evenings and Sun.)
					Discount Rate (Late night)

The above times refer to Japan time, not the time in the country called.

Telegrams: The following KDD office is open 24 hours a day throughout the year and handle telegrams, facsimiles and phototelegrams, and has booth's for ISD calls and telex.

Tokyo Telegraph Office   Tel.(03)3344-5151

※From any part of Japan, please call this number.

BUSINESS HOURS

Banks: Banks are open 9:00 a.m. — 3:00 p.m., Monday through Friday. Closed on Saturdays, Sundays, and national holidays.

Government and Business Offices: Most are open from 8:30 or 9:30 a.m. to 5 or 6 p.m. Monday through Friday and until noon on Saturdays, although more and more business offices are closed on Saturdays, Sundays and national holidays.

Post Offices: 9 a.m. to 5 p.m. Monday through Fribay. Closed on Saturday, Sunday and national holidays. Main post offices also conduct postal transactions (excluding postal savings, etc.) on Saturday 9 a.m. to 5 p.m. and Sunday mornings.

Restaurants: Hours vary from place to place but most are open for lunch and dinner every day.

Shops: Department stores are open 10:00 a.m. to 7:00 p.m., even on Sundays and national holidays. Department stores have a regular holiday once a week, the day varying between each store.

REST ROOM

Department stores and hotel lobbies contain toilet facilities without rest room attendants. Most of the time these are Japanese squat toilets but you can find Western-style stool toilets in large office buildings and similar places.

LOST AND FOUND

If you leave your bag on a station bench or somewhere, you don't have to assume it's lost forever. You can go back to where you left it and it will probably still be there. If not, go to the Station Master's Office or to the nearest police station.

INFORMATION OFFICE

TIC's (Tourist Information Centers), staffed by multilingual personnel, offer various information services for visitors from abroad. They prepare free maps and booklets. Sightseeing, shopping and dining information and all other TIC services are free of charge. For more information see P155.

USEFUL TELEPHONE NUMBERS

AIRLINES

TOKYO☎03, OSAKA☎06

Airport Information
(Narita)☎0476-32-2800
(Osaka)☎06-856-6781
Aeroflot Soviet Airlines(SU)
☎03-3434-9671
Air Canada(AC)   ☎03-3585-4635
Air France(AF)   ☎06-201-5161
Air India   (AI)   ☎06-264-1781
Air Lanka(UL)   ☎03-3573-4261
Air New Zealand(NZ)   ☎06-212-8990
Alitalia Airlines(AZ) ☎06-341-3951
All Nippon Airways(NH)
☎06 372-1212
American Airlines(AA) ☎06-264-6308
British Airways(BA)   ☎06-345-2761
Cathay Pacific Airways(CX)
☎06-245-6731
Canadian Airlines International(CP)
☎06-346-5591
China Airlines(CI)   ☎03-3436-1661
Continental Airlines(CO)
☎03-3592-1631
Delta Air Lines(DL)   ☎06-243-2525
Egypt Air(MS)   ☎06-341-1575
Finnair(AY)   ☎06-363-0270
Garuda Indonesian Airways(GA)
☎06-445-6985
General Administration of Civil Aviation
of China(CA)   ☎06-946-1702
Iran Air(IR)   ☎03-3586-2101
Iraqi Ariways(IA)   ☎03-3264-5503
Japan Airlines(JL)   ☎06-203-1212
Japan Asia Airways(EG)
☎06-223-2222
KLM Royal Dutch Airlines(KL)
☎06-345-6691
Korean Air Lines(KE) ☎06-264-3311
Lufthansa German Airlines(LH)
☎06-345-0231
Malaysian Airline System(MH)
☎06-245-7123
Air Nippon(EL)
☎06-374-5131
Northwest Orient Airlines(NW)
☎06-228-0747
Olympic Airways(OA)
☎03-3583-1911
Pakistan International Airlines(PK)
☎06-341-3106
Philippine Airlines(PR)
☎06-444-2541
Quantas Airways(QF)   ☎0120-207020

Sabena Belgian World Airlines(SN)
☎06-341-8081
Scandinavian Airlines System(SK)
☎06-348-0211
Singapore Airlines(SQ)
☎06-364-0881
Swiss Air Transport(SR)
☎06-345-7851
Thai Airways International(TG)
☎06-202-5161
Sabena Belgian World Airlines(SN)
☎06-341-8081
Japan Air System(JD)
☎06-345-2828
Transworld Airlines(TW)
☎06-365-7177
United Airlines(UA)   ☎06-271-5951
UTA French Airlines(UT)
☎06-201-5161
Varig Brazilian Airlines(RG)
☎03-5269-2680

FOREIGN DIPLOMATIC OFFICES

C: Consulate
CG: Consulate-General
HC: Honorary Consulate

OSAKA☎06

American CG   ☎315-5900
Australian CG   ☎271-7071
Austrian HCG   ☎241-3011
Belgian HC   ☎773-5289
British CG   ☎231-3355
Chad HC   ☎231-5841
Chilean HC   ☎359-1123
Chinese CG   ☎445-9481
Danish HC   ☎346-1285
El Salvador HC   ☎348-3183
Finnish HCG   ☎361-0938
French CG   ☎946-6181
Gabon C   ☎208-5400
Guatemala HC   ☎761-7206
India CG   ☎261-7299
Italian CG   ☎949-1619
Korean CG   ☎213-1401
Mexican HC   ☎343-0050
Pakistani HC   ☎266-2007
Portuguese HC   ☎267-6090
Singapore C   ☎261-5131
Soviet CG   ☎848-3452
Spanish HC   ☎661-9068
Sri Lanka HCG   ☎338-0230
Swiss CG   ☎344-7671
Thai HCG   ☎243-5563
Turkish HCG   ☎653-3577

KOBE☎078
Federal Republic of Germany CG
☎232-1212
Indonesia CG ☎321-1654
Netherlandish CG ☎232-3400

FOREIGN BANKS
OSAKA☎06
Abn. Amro Bank N.V. ☎243-6061
Bank of America ☎231-8891
Korea Exchange Bank ☎263-2111
Citibank, N.A. ☎227-5611
Hong Kong & Shanghai Banking
☎231-8701

CHURCHES
KYOTO☎075
Japan Baptist Church ☎231-1351
St. Francis Church ☎231-4785
St. Mary's Church ☎771-2581
Heian Church ☎721-2589
Rakuyo Church ☎231-1276
NARA☎0742
Nara Catholic Church ☎26-2094
OSAKA☎06
Christ Church Cathedral ☎581-5061
Osaka Christian Center ☎762-7701
KOBE☎078
Nakayamate Catholic Church
☎221-4682
St. Michael's Cathedral ☎341-1085
Kobe Eiko Church ☎331-2286

HOSPITALS
KYOTO☎075
Kyoto City Hospital ☎311-5311
Japan Baptist Hospital ☎781-5191
Kyoto University Hospital☎751-3111
Koyto Prefectural University Hospital
☎251-5111
NARA☎0742
Nara National Hospital ☎24-1251
OSAKA☎06
Osaka National Hospital ☎942-1331
Yodogawa Christian Hospital
☎322-2250
Osaka Prefectural Hospital
☎692-1201
KOBE☎078
Kobe Kaisei Hospital ☎871-5201
Kobe Central Municipal Hospital
☎302-4321
Palmore Hospital ☎321-6000

LIBRARIES
KYOTO☎075
Kyoto Prefectural Library
☎771-0069
OSAKA☎06
Osaka American Center ☎315-5970
Osaka Prefectural Library
☎203-0474

EMERGENCY
Police ☎110
Fire Dept. & Ambulance ☎119

INFORMATION
Operator assisted Calls ☎0051
(4 digit number from anywhere in Japan)
KYOTO☎075
Kyoto City Government ☎752-0215
Kyoto City Office ☎222-3111
Kyoto Office of the Imperial Household
Agency ☎211-1211
Kyoto Tourist Information Center
(JNTO) ☎371-5649
Teletourist Service(taped information
Service of current events)
☎361-2911
OTSU☎0775
Otsu City Information ☎22-3830
Otsu City Office ☎23-1234
NARA☎0742
Nara City Tourist Center ☎22-3900
Nara City Office ☎34-1111
OSAKA☎06
Osaka City Office ☎208-8181
Osaka Municipal Tourist Information
Office ☎345-2189
Osaka Tourist Association
☎208-8955
Osaka Tourist Information Center
☎305-3311
Tourist Information Service
☎941-9200
KOBE☎078
Kobe City Office ☎331-8181
Kobe International Tourist Association
☎303-1010
Ise☎0596
Ise City Office ☎23-1111

PRINCIPAL JTB OFFICE
Ise Office ☎0596-28-7171
Kyoto Office ☎075-341-7141
Nara Office ☎0742-23-2525
Osaka Umeda Office ☎06-365-1134
Kobe Sannomiya Office
☎078-231-4118
Otsu Office ☎0775-22-4853

155

FESTIVALS AND ANNUAL EVENTS IN THE KINKI REGION

■JANUARY
1: Okera-Mairi at Yasaka Shrine(Kyoto)／A herb called *okera* is burnt in lanterns as an offering to the enshrined gods, starting at 8: OO p.m on New Year's Eve. Torches lit in the flames of the lantern are taken home and used to cook the first meal of the New Year.

1-3: Ōbukuchajuyo at Rokuharamitsuji Temple (Kyoto)／Green tea believed to ward off illness is presented to visitors.

4: Kemarihajime at Shimogamo Shrine(Kyoto)／the traditional *kemari* (ball-game) is performed.

9-11: Tōka Ebisu at Imamiya Ebisu Shrine(Osaka)／Thousands make appeals for prosperity to *Ebisu*, the god of commerce. *Fukuzasa*, a charm made of bamboo grass which brings success in business, is sold.

14: Doyadoya at Shitennōji Temple(Osaka)／Two groups of men clad only in loincloths jostle each other. The winning group is said to be blessed with good harvests.

15: Wakakusayama-yaki on Mt. Wakakusa(Nara)／Priests from Tōdaiji and Kōfukuji Temples light the dry grass on Mt. Wakakusa, the whole mountain is covered in flames, making a brilliant spectacle.

■FEBRUARY
3: Setsubun: Onioishiki at Kōfukuji Temple(Nara)／*Setsubun* marks the last day of winter. A short play is held featuring 6 goblins with clubs and the god, *Bishamonten*.

25: Baikasai at Kitano Temmangū Shrine(Kyoto)／An open-air tea ceremony and memorial rites for the shrine deity are held under Japanese apricot trees in full bloom.

■MARCH
1-14: Shunie(Omizutori) at Tōdaiji Temple(Nara)／See p.108

■APRIL
1-30: Miyako Odori at the Gion Kōbu Kaburenjō Theater(Kyoto)／Traditional Kyoto dancing performed by *geiko* and *maiko*, accompanied by traditional instruments.

1-7: Hinaeshiki at Hokkeji Temple(Nara)／30 images of *Zenzaidōji*, donated by devotees, are displayed in front of the Main Hall.

2: Matsuno-o Shrine Reitaisai at Matsuno-o

Shrine(Kyoto)／Traditional *kyōgen* and *yōkyoku* music performances.

2nd Sat. and Sun.: Ochamori at Saidaiji Temple(Nara)／ An amusing tea ceremony using giant-size cups.

2nd Sun: Yasurai Matsuri at Imamiya Shrine(Kyoto)／ Held to placate the spirits of plagues that, in bygone days, people suffered after spring. Children with red hair, others dressed as demons and goblins make a procession.

2nd Sun.: Taikō Hanami Gyōretsu at Daigoji Temple(Kyoto)／A re-enactment, in Momoyama era costume, of the *Daigo-no-Hanami* (Cherry-blossom) party, held here in 1598 by *Hideyoshi Toyotomi*.

21-29: Mibu Kyōgen at Mibudera Temple(Kyoto)／Pantomime farces which date back to the Kamakura era.

29: Kyokusui-no-en at Jōnangū Shrine(Kyoto)／Re-enactment of an event dating from the Heian era. A poet writes a short poem(*tanka*) in the time it takes for a *sake* cup to pass by on the stream in front of him.

■**MAY**

1-24: Kamogawa Odori at Pontochō Kaburenjō Theater(Kyoto)／A dance performance by *geiko* and *maiko*, similar to the Miyako Odori.

15: Aoi Matsuri at Kamigamo and Shimogamo Shrines(Kyoto)／See p.69

3rd Sat. and Sun.: Kobe Matsuri on Flower Road(Kobe)／ A colorful carnival with foreign residents participating.

■**JUNE**

1-2: Takigi-Noh at Heian Shrine(Kyoto)／A torchlight *Noh* performance held on an outdoor stage.

2: Kibune Matsuri at Kibune Shrine(Kyoto)／Also known as *Itadori Matsuri*. A portable shrine is paraded.

20: Takekiri-e at Kuruma Temple(Kyoto)／A bamboo-cutting ceremony to divine the success or failure of the year's harvests.

■**JULY**

1-29: Gion Matsuri at Yasaka Shrine(Kyoto)／See p.54

7: Kaerutobi at Kompusen Temple(Nara)／Performers in frog costumes parade through the town.

24, 25: Tenjin Matsuri at Temmangū Shrine(Osaka)／ See p.130

13-16: (by the lunar calender) Urabon-e at Kanteibyō(Kobe)／A bustling Chinese festival with bells and bowls used to make lots of noise.

157

■AUGUST

7: Daibutsu Ominugui at Daibutsuden Hall, Tōdaiji Temple(Nara) / A ritual cleaning of the Great Buddha.

16: Daimonji Gozan Okuribi on Gozan, the 'Five Mountains' (Kyoto) / See p.72

23, 24: Sentō Kuyō at Nembutsuji Temple(Kyoto) / Lighted torches are placed on the stone effigies in the grounds to comfort the souls of the departed.

■SEPTEMBER

1st Sun.: Hassaku Matsuri at Matsuno-o Shrine(Kyoto) / A festival petitioning for favorable weather and harvests, which includes sacred sumo matches.

Harvest Moon: Kangetsu-no-Yūbe at Daikakuji Temple(Kyoto) / Moon-viewing from elegant traditional boats on the river.

■OCTOBER

1-5: Zuiki Matsuri at Kitano Temmangū Shrine(Kyoto) / A festival expressing gratitude to the gods for the year's good harvests. Decorated floats parade through the streets. The float carrying the portable shrine is made of *zuiki*, stalks of the taro.

Mid-Oct.—early Nov.: Shika-no-Tsunokiri at Kasuga Shrine(Nara) / An event beld to cut off the antlers of Nara Park's deer, to prevent injuries to people.

Mid-Oct. —early Nov.: Shōsōin Exhibition at Nara National Museum(Nara) / Exhibition of the art treasures stored in the Shōsōin.

22: Jidai Matsuri (Festival of the Ages). Heian Shrine(Kyoto) / See P.63

22: Kurama-no-Himatsuri (Great Fire Festival) at Yuki Shrine(Kyoto) / Participants carrying torches parade through the town.

■NOVEMBER

2nd Sun: Momiji Matsuri in Arashiyama Hill(Kyoto) / Temples and shrines near the Ōi River put out their boats with people in 10th C costumes aboard, in appreciation of the beautiful red and yellow maples on the mountainside.

■DECEMBER

15-18: Kasuga Wakamiya Matsuri at Kasuga Wakamiya Shrine(Nara) / A procession, similar to that of the Jidai Matsuri, parades around the shrine and performances of *gagaku* and *bugaku*, Japanese classical music, are given.

PACKAGE TOURS TO KYOTO AND ENVIRONS

JTB PACKAGE TOURS (SUNRISE TOURS)
■ *Tours in Kyoto*

KYOTO MORNING TOUR
■ *Departure:* Daily 8:20 a.m. –around 12:00 p.m.
■ *Fare:* ¥5,000 (Child: ¥4,000)
■ *Tour Highlights:* Nijō Castle, Golden Pavilion, Kyoto Imperial Palace(Higashi-Honganji Temple), Kyoto Handicraft Center.

KYOTO AFTERNOON TOUR
■ *Departure:* Daily 2:00 p.m. –around 5:30 p.m.
■ *Fare:* ¥5,000 (Child ¥4,000)
■ *Tour Highlights:* Heian Shrine, Sanjūsangendō, Kiyomizu Temple.

KYOTO 1 DAY
■ *Departure:* Daily 8:20 a.m. —around 5:30 p.m.
■ *Fare:* ¥10,600 (Child ¥8,500)
■ *Tour Highlights:* Nijō Castle, Golden Pavilion, Kyoto Imperial Palace, (Higashi-Honganji Temple,) Kyoto Handicraft Center, Heian-jingū Shrine, Sanjūsangendō Hall, Kiyomizu Temple.

KYOTO SPECIAL NIGHT TOUR
■ *Departure:* Every Tuesday, Thursday and Saturday (March through November) 6:00 p.m.–around 10:00 p.m.
■ *Fare:* ¥10,000 (Dinner included.)
■ *Tour Highlights:* Being a guest at Tea Ceremony and Zen-style Tempura supper at a Japanese inn. Enjoy various kinds of Japanese traditional arts at Gion Corner.
■ *Tours in Nara*

NARA AFTERNOON TOUR
■ *Departure:* Daily 1:00 p.m.–around 6:00～7:00 p.m. except Jannuary
■ *Fare:* ¥5,700 (Child ¥4,700)
■ *Tour Highlights:* Tōdaiji Temple, Dear Park, Kasuga Shrine.

159

KYOTO & NARA 1 DAY

■*Departure:* Daily 8:20 a.m.–around 6:30～7:30 p.m. except Jan. & Dec. 31
■*Fare:* 11,500 (Child ¥9,000)
■*Tour Highlights:* KYOTO MORNING TOUR + NARA AFTERNOON TOUR

POTTERY MAKING & KIMONO

■*Departure:* Daily 8:20 a.m.–around 12:00 p.m. (Apr, through Dec.)
■*Fare:* 12,000(Child:¥8,000)
■*Tour Highlits:* Own painting on Kiyomizu Pottery and tring to put on a Kimono.

ISE & PEARL ISLAND FULL DAY TOUR

■*Departure:* Daily (March through November)
■*Fare:* ¥24,800(Child ¥18,900)(Lnuch included.)
■*Tour Highlights:* From Kyoto Station or Osaka Uehommachi Station to Toba. See Mikimoto Pearl Island, exhibitions of pearl cultivation and demonstrations by women pearl divers. Seafood lunch at Toba Hotel International. Visit Ise Jingū Shrine.

● *Information and Reservations*

You can call any of the companies listed below or ask at major hotels in the city.
Japan Travel Bureau Sunrise Tour Center
(Tokyo) ☎03-3276-7777 (☎03-3432-1111 at night)
(Kyoto)   ☎075-341-1413
Fujita Travel Service(FTS)   ☎075-222-0121
Hankyū Express International   ☎06-373-5471
Hato Bus   ☎03-3276-7777
Japan Gray Line   ☎075-492-9430

TRAVEL
LIFE

❖

LODGING

As befits an international tourist city, Kyoto abounds in comfortable hotels and cozy traditional inns offering first-class service and quiet hospitality.

WESTERN STYLE HOTELS

● DELUXE AND FIRST CLASS HOTELS

There is no official grading system but the standard of services and facilities are exceptionally high at these hotels. They provide excellent restaurants, shopping arcades (including dutyfree), travel information counters and direct airport connections. Some hotels also offer "executive salons" which allow guests to utilize various secretarial services.

● BUSINESS HOTELS

These hotels were developed to accommodate travelling businessmen on a modest budget. They are clean and conveniently located but do not offer room or other similar services. There are usually restaurants and vending machines on the premises.

● YOUTH HOSTELS

For tight-budget travel, youth hostels are recommended. Some require membership in the Japan Youth Hostels or International Youth Hostel Federation but there are also those that waive these requirements. The YMCA and YWCA also offer inexpensive lodging.

● PENSIONS

These are a more recent type of western style accommodation. The name is borrowed from the French and pensions feature a homely atmosphere and hearty meals. The average price is ¥6,000 per person with 2 meals.

● HINTS ON STAYING AT HOTELS

1. Room charges only cover lodging and service.
2. Check-in: 11 a.m. or noon. (4 p.m. for business hotels.)
3. Check-out: 11 a.m. or noon. (10 a.m. for business hotels.)
4. A service charge of 10% to 15% is added to your bill. At some hotels tips of ¥200 - ¥300 per piece are given to bellboys for assistance with baggage.
5. *Yukata* (light cotton kimono) are provided to wear when sleeping or relaxing in

your room.

JAPANESE STYLE LODGINGS

● RYOKAN

Staying at a *ryokan* is probably the closest a visitor will come to traditional Japanese life. The rooms are laid with *tatami* (reed mat). Bathrooms are often communal. Room rates in ryokan range from ¥5,000 all the way up to ¥60,000 per person and are usually quoted on a basis of 2 or more per room. This includes dinner and breakfast.

The meals are somewhat elaborate affairs featuring the local specialties. Often, the food will be brought to your room. A 6% tax and a 10%–15% service charge will be added to your check. There are approximately 90,000 ryokans in Japan and over 2,000 belong to the Japan Ryokan Association.

● *ECONOMY INNS*

There are increasing numbers of non-Japanese visitors at these low-priced ryokans and the members of the Japanese Inn Group offer worry-free lodging for all kinds of travelers. Room rates average ¥4,000, excluding meals.

● *MINSHUKU*

Minshuku in something like a guest house. It is operated by families so the atmosphere in homey and relaxed. The rates are usually around ¥4,500 which includes 2 meals. Toilet articles and other amenities usually available at hotels and ryokans are not provided.

● *HINTS ON STAYING AT A RYOKAN*

1. Check-in: Around 4 p.m. Check - out: Around 10 a.m.
2. When you arrive, you leave your shoes at the entrance and step into the slippers that will lay waiting. These slippers are worn while walking around inside the *ryokan* but never on the *tatami*.
3. A maid will serve tea, bring your meal to your room, and lay out your *futon* (bedding) at night.
4. You will be provided with a *yukata* (light cotton kimono) or a padded *dotera*, depending on the season. These may be worn anywhere inside the *ryokan* but are not usually worn on the street.
5. Since a service charge is included in the check, no tipping is necessary.
6. Except in some modern ryokans, bathing is communal (but separated by sex). There will be baskets to leave your clothes. Always wash in the plentiful hot water provided outside the tub and be careful

not to contaminate the bath with soap, shampoo, etc.

7. Most rooms do not have keys so leave your valuables at the front desk or in the safe provided in your room.

HOME VISITS

If visitors are interested in observing Japanese home life, the Home-Visit Program offers them an opportunity to visit typical families in the city. Families are selected by the Mayor of Kyoto and visitors can enjoy a friendly chat over tea with family members for a few hours, and see what real Japanese home-life is like. There is no charge for home-visits, however, visitors usually take a small gift for the hostess, such as candy or fruit. All expenses for transportation and interpreting services if used, are borne by visitors. Applications for home-visits are accepted 2 days in advance at the Tourist Section, Kyoto City Government.

RESERVATIONS

It is best to make reservations as early as possible. During the peak travel seasons (the summer or the Christmas season) finding a vacancy can be impossible.

SERVICE CHARGE & TAXES

A 6% tax is added when total room and meal charges exceed ¥10,000 per person per night. At first class and deluxe hotels, a 10% service charge is added to obviate the need for tipping. At *ryokans*, where each room has a maid, a 15% service charge will usually be added. There is no service charge at business hotels, youth hostels, pensions, economy inns or *minshuku*.

● Unit: in hundreds of yen.
● Prices for hotels show twin room charge only.
● Prices for business hotels show single room charge only.
● Prices for inns show the charge for one person to stay in a twin room including two meals.
● H. means Hotel, R. means Ryokan.

Name	R.C.	address	Tel.

〈**KYOTO**〉 ☎**075** (The word 'shi' means 'city' and is used with all the city names below except Kyoto.)

● Major Hotels

Name	R.C.	address	Tel.
H. Fujita Kyoto	185-325	Kamogawa-Nijō-Ōhashi-Nishizume, Nakagyō-ku	☎222-1511
H. Keihan Kyoto	161-185	31, Higashikujō-Nishisan-nōchō, Minami-ku	☎661-0321
H. New Hankyū Kyoto	160-325	Shiokōjidōri-Kyōtoeki-shōmen, Shimogyō-ku	☎343-5300
H. New Kyoto	143-269	Horikawa-Marutamachi-kado, Kamigyō-ku	☎801-2111

164

Holiday-inn Kyoto	148-189	36, Takano-Nishibirakichō, Sakyō-ku	☎721-3131
International H. Kyoto	180-300	Horikawadōri Nijō-mae, Nakagyō-ku	☎222-1111
Kyoto Century H.	235-297	Higashinotōindōri, Shiokōji-sagaru, Shimogyō-ku	☎351-0111
		Shichijo-sagaru, Shimogyō-ku	☎351-0111
Kyoto Grand H.	191-300	Horikawa-Shiokōji, Shimogyō-ku	☎341-2311
Kyoto Zennikcū H.	231-360	Nijōjō-mae, Horilcawa-dōri, Nakagyō-ku	☎231-1155
Kyoto Palace-side H.	120-156	Karasumadōri-Shimotachiuri-agaru, Kamigyō-ku	☎431-8171
Kyoto Park H.	172-238	644-2, Sanjūsangendō-Mawarichō, Higashiyama-ku	☎525-3111
Kyoto Royal H.	190-415	Kawaramachi-Sanjō-agaru, Nakagyō-ku	☎223-1234
Kyoto Takaragaike Prince H.	279-299	Takaragaike, Sakyō-ku	☎712-1111
Kyoto Tokyu H.	189-571	Horikawadōri-Gojō-sagaru, Shimogyō-ku	☎341-2411
Kyoto Tower H.	135-182	Karasumadōri-Shichijō-sagaru, Shimogyō-ku	☎361-3211
Miyako H.	214-426	Sanjō-Keage, Higashiyama-ku	☎771-7111
New Miyako H.	170-250	17, Nishi-Kujoin-machi, Minami-ku	☎661-7111

● **Major Ryokans**

Chikiriya	220-400	Takoyakushi-Tominokōji-Nishi-iru, Nakagyō-ku	☎221-1281
Hiiragiya	300-800	Fuyachō Anekōji-agaru, Nakagyō-ku	☎221-1136
Hifumi	100-150	Akezu-dōri, Shichijō-sagaru, Shimogyō-ku	☎371-1238
Izutsuan	120-150	Higashinotōin-dōri, Shōmen-sagaru	☎371-1574
Kaneiwarō Bekkan	165-324	Kiyamachidōri-Matsubara-sagaru, Shimogyō-ku	☎351-5010
Masuya	120-240	Shinfuya-chō-dōri, Niōmon-sagaru	☎771-3066
Seikōrō	186-415	467, Tonyamachi-Gojō-sagaru, Higashiyama-ku	☎561-0771
Sumiya	350-650	Fuyachō-Sanjō-sagaru, Nakagyō-ku	☎221-2188
Tawaraya	288-368	Fuyachō-Anekōji-agaru, Nakagyō-ku	☎211-5566

● **Business Hotels**

H. Rich Kyoto	110-165	Gojō-agaru, Kawaramachidōri, Shimogyō-ku	☎341-1131
Kyoto Garden H.	73	Minami-iru, Oike, Muromachidōri, Nakagyō-ku	☎255-2000
Kyoto Gion H.	155-290	555, Minamigawa, Giommachi, Higashiyama-ku	☎551-2111
Sun Hotel Kyoto	83	Sanjō-sagaru, Kawaramachidōri, Nakagyō-ku	☎241-3351

● **Youth Hostels**

| Higashiyama Youth Hostel | 40-55 | 112, Shirakawabashi-Gokenchō, Sanjōdōri, Higashiyama-ku | ☎761-8135 |
| Kitayama Youth Hostel | 42 | Kōetsuji-hotori, Takagamine, Kita-ku | ☎492-5345 |

● **Pensions**

Pension Higashiyama Gion	70	Sanjō-sagaru, Shirakawasuji, Higashiyama-ku	☎882-1181
Pension Sagano	82	26-4, Yamagoe-Higashimachi, Ukyō-ku	☎881-2310
Pension Shimogamo	78	20, Shimogamo-Kamikawaramachi, Sakyō-ku	☎711-0180

● **Minshuku**

| Kyoto Minshuku Reservation Center | | 7F, ON Bldg., Kyotoeki-mae, Shimogyō-ku | ☎351-4547 |

⟨NARA⟩ ☎0742

● **Major Hotel**

| Nara H. | 239-253 | 1096, Takabatakechō, Nara-shi | ☎26-3300 |

165

● Major Ryokans

Heijō	160-300	728, Kawakamichō, Nara-shi	☎22-3142
Kasuga H.	270-400	40, Noboriōjichō, Nara-shi	☎22-4031
Kikusuiro	311-457	1130, Takabatakechō, Nara-shi	☎23-2001
Shiki-tei	305-503	Ichinotorii-yoko, Narakōennai, Nara-shi	☎22-5531

● Business Hotels

H. Sun-Route Nara	130-173	1110, Takabatake-Bodaichō, Nara-shi	☎22-5151

● Youth Hostel

Nara Youth Hostel	22	Sōgōundōkōennai, 1716, Hōrenchō, Nara-shi	☎22-1334

〈OSAKA〉 ☎06
● Major Hotels

H. Hanshin	200-320	2-3-30, Umeda, Kita-ku, Osaka-shi	☎344-1661
H. New Hankyū	190-440	1-1-35, Shibata, Kita-ku, Osaka-shi	☎372-5101
H. New Otani Osaka	300-700	1-4-1, Shiromi, Chūō-ku, Osaka-shi	☎941-1111
H. Nikkō Osaka	270-3000	1-3-3, Nishi-Shinsaibashi, Chūō-ku, Osaka-shi	☎244-1111
H. Osaka Castle	119-135	1-1, Kyō-machi, Temmabashi, Chūō-ku, Osaka-shi	☎942-2401
H. Osaka Grand	230-780	2-3-18, Nakanoshima, Kita-ku, Osaka-shi	☎202-1212
H. Plaza	240-900	2-2-49, Ōyodo-Minami, Ōyodo-ku, Osaka-shi	☎453-1111
Holiday-Inn Nankai	235-1000	2-5-15, Shinsaibashisuji, Chūō-ku, Osaka-shi	☎213-8281
Osaka Airport H.	187-242	3-555, Hotarugaike-Nishimachi, Toyonaka-shi	☎855-4621
Osaka Hilton International	305-445	1-8-8, Umeda, Kita-ku, Osaka-shi	☎347-7111
Osaka Terminal H.	190-330	3-1-1, Umeda, Kita-ku, Osaka-shi	☎344-1235
Osaka Zennikkū H. Sheraton	270-2700	1-3-1, Dōjimahama, Kita-ku, Osaka-shi	☎347-1112
Royal H.	270-900	5-3-68, Nakanoshima, Kita-ku, Osaka-shi	☎448-1121
Senri Hankyū H.	170-400	2-1-D-1, Shinsenri-Higashimachi, Toyonaka-shi	☎872-2211

● Major Ryokans

H. Hishitomi	100-150	1-4-8, Hommachi, Chūō-ku, Osaka-shi	☎261-1112
Kaneyoshi Ryokan	150-250	3-12, Sōemonchō, Chūō-ku, Osaka-shi	☎211-6337
Ryokan Kitahachi	130-160	7-16, Dōyamachō, Kita-ku, Osaka-shi	☎361-2078
Yamatoya Honten	130-180	2-17-4, Shimanouchi, Chūō-ku, Osaka-shi	☎211-3587

〈KOBE〉 ☎078

H. Kobe	140-200	5-2-31, Kumochichō, Chūō-ku, Kobe-shi	☎221-5431
Kobe Gajoen H.	131-170	8-4-23, Shimoyamatedōri, Chūō-ku, Kobe-shi	☎341-0301
Kobe Portpia H.	220-2500	6-10-1,Minatojima-Nakamachi, Chūō-ku, Kobe-shi	☎302-1111
Kōbe Tokyu Inn	170	6-1-5, Kumoi-dōri, Chūō-ku, Kōbe-shi	☎291-0109
Oriental H.	230-260	25, Kyōmachi, Chūō-ku, Kōbe-shi	☎331-8111
Rokkō Oriental H.	209-231	1878, Nishitaniyama, Rokkōsanchō, Nadaku, Kobe-shi	☎891-0333
Rokkō	H.120-350	1034, Minamirokkō, Rokkōsanshō Nadaku, kobe-shi	☎891-0301
Takarazuka H.	190-1000	1-46, Umenochō, Takarazuka-shi	☎0797-87-1151

DINING

Kyoto has a multitude of delicious specialty dishes and Osaka has always been popular with gourmets. The Kansai region generally has been a area where numerous dishes and ways of preparation have been developed and popularized.

RESTAURANTS

● RYŌTEI

Top-class restaurants in Japan serve the best of the country's dishes in elegant surroundings with quiet, discreet service. *Ryōtei* are traditional restaurants in this class and most require reservations. Some will only serve guests introduced through established customers.

● INEXPENSIVE RESTAURANTS

There is a limitless variety of friendly, inexpensive restaurants to be found on almost every street and alley in Japan. The plastic samples in the display cases, which are accurate replicas of what you are actually served, will help you decide what to order.

JAPANESE DELICACIES

● TEMPURA

Introduced by the Portuguese in the 16th century, *tempura* has been refined over the years and the result is a feather-light batter deep-fried in the purest vegetable oil. Numerous ingredients are used, popular ones being shrimp, squid, eggplant, and sweet potato. The *tempura* is dipped into a special soy sauce before eating.

● SUSHI

One of the best-known Japanese dishes, *sushi* (raw fish on vinegared rice) is made to order in all but the cheapest shops so you can point to the desired topping in the glass case in front of the counter when ordering.

● SUKIYAKI AND SHABU-SHABU

Sukiyaki consists of thin strips of beef, sliced green onion, *tōfu*, vegetables and *shirataki* (a gelatinous noodle), all cooked at your table. When ready, take a portion with your chopsticks and dip it in your bowl of beaten raw egg.

For *shabu-shabu* you do the cooking! Thinly sliced beef is dipped in a pot of boiling water and vegetables.

● TONKATSU

This is deep-fried, crumbed pork cutlets. A *tonkatsu tei-*

167

shoku (set meal) will probably include *tonkatsu*, shredded cabbage, tomato, *miso* soup, and rice.

● NOODLES

Noodles were introduced into Japan from China, and there are 3 basic types: *soba* (buckwheat noodles), *udon* (wheat noodles), rāmen or *chūka soba* (thin egg noodles). Noodles are an extremely popular and generally inexpensive dish.

● KAISEKI RYŌRI

Traditionally served as a simple light meal before a tea ceremony, *Kaiseki* cuisine is now available in restaurants. A full course includes small portions of numerous dishes all beautifully presented. The best fish and vegetables are selected and cooked with care taken not to destroy the original taste and flavor. The focus is aesthetic, with emphasis placed on shape and color, so *Kaiseki* tends to be expensive, but is a true feast for the eyes.

● SHŌJIN RYŌRI

In Buddhism, *Shōjin* means abstinence and purification and is the name given to a type of vegetarian meal prepared by Buddhist priests of the *Zen* sect. Ingredients include seasonal vegetables, noodles, *tōfu* and *yuba* and everything is served in vermillion laquerware dishes. The true pleasure of *Shōjin ryōri* is being able to appreciate the beauty of the temple garden and surroundings while enjoying the meal.

● KYŌ RYŌRI

The most elegant and refined dishes in Japan are said to be Kyoto's own local dishes, which originated as imperial cuisine and have been strongly influenced by Buddhism. Seasoning is used sparingly so that the original taste can be savored and emphasis is placed on careful arrangement and presentation.

● YUDŌFU

Eating *Yudōfu* consists of boiling small cubes of *tōfu* in water and then dipping them in soy sauce with spices. The quality of Kyoto's water adds to the *tōfu's* taste. Kyoto has several famous wholesale stores such as **Morika** which supply high quality *tōfu* to shops and restaurants.

● UDONSUKI

This dish resembles *sukiyaki* with a variety of ingredients boiled in a dish including chicken, fish, vegetables, *yuba* and thick noodles.

● KOBE BEEF

As a port city, Kobe has long been influenced by foreign culture and cuisine. So it's not surprising that Kobe produces its own high quality beef, which is even exported overseas. As often happens with foods introduced from abroad, novel ways of preparing and cooking beef have originated in Kobe, such as *shabu-shabu* and raw beef dishes.

INTERNATIONAL CUISINE

Kyoto, being a tourist city, abounds in French, Italian and other European restaurants catering to western food lovers. Kobe, however, surpasses Kyoto in the variety of foreign cuisine available and has numerous established restaurants offering genuine, original dishes, including

Greek, Russian, Spanish and Indian cuisine.

ALCOHOL

Both domestic and imported liquor is available at hotels, restaurants and nightclubs among other places. Imported liquor is naturally more expensive. Whisky is very popular in Japan and the local distillations are quite good. Japanese beer, both lager and draught, is generally excellent. *Sake* is brewed from rice and is served warm or over ice. *Shōchū* is becoming increasingly popular, especially with the nation's young people. It is lighter than *sake* and is distilled from rice, wheat.

169

Name	address	Tel.

〈KYOTO〉 ☎075

● *Japanese*

Azekura (Soba)	30, Kamigamo-Okamotochō, Kita-ku	☎701-0161
Daikokuya (Soba)	Nishi-Kiyamachi-Takoyakushi-Nishi-iru, Nakagyōku	☎221-2818
Daitokuji Ikkyū (Shōjin-ryōri)	20, Murasakino-Daitokujimae, Kita-ku	☎493-0019
Gombei (Udon)	254, Kitagawa, Gionmachi, Higashiyama-ku	☎561-3350
Hiranoya (Imobō)	Chion-in-minami-monmae, Maruyamakōen, Higashiyama-ku	☎561-1603
Hirokawa (Eel)	48, Sagatenryūji-Kitatsukurimichichō, Ukyō-ku	☎871-5226
Hyōmasa (Kyō-ryōri)	Nishi-Kiyamachi-Shijō-agaru, Nakagyō-ku	☎221-4424
Hyōtei (Kansai-ryōri)	35, Nanzenji-Kusakawachō, Sakyō-ku	☎771-4116
Ippeijaya (Kaburamushi)	Miyagawasuji, Higashiyama-ku	☎561-4052
Izuu (Sushi)	367, Kiyomotochō, Yasakashinji, Higashiyama-ku	☎561-0750
Izusen (Shōjin-ryōri)	Murasakino-Daitokujimachi-Daijiin-nai, Kita-ku	☎491-6665
Jūbei (Sushi)	Nawateshimbashi-agaru, Higashiyama-ku	☎561-2698
Junsei (Yudōfu)	60, Nanzenji-Kusakawachō, Sakyō-ku	☎761-2311
Kanoko Honten (Sukiyaki)	Kiyamachi-Shijō-sagaru, Shimogyō-ku	☎351-2081
Kawaramachiya Misoka-an (Soba)	Sanjō-agaru, Fuyachōdōri, Nakagyō-ku	☎221-2525
Kicchō (Kaiseki-ryōri)	58, Sagatenryūji-Susukinobabachō, Ukyō-ku	☎881-1101

Kikunoi (Kaiseki-ryōri)
459, Shimogawaradōri-Shimogawarachō, Higashiyama-ku ☎561-0015
Kikusui (Kaiseki-ryōri) 31, Nanzenji-Fukuchichō,Sakyō-ku ☎771-4101
Kirisoba (Soba) 3, Sagatenryūji-Susukinobabachō, Ukyō-ku ☎861-0728
Kōetsujaya (Kyō-ryōri) 46-2, Takagamine-Kōetsuchō, Kita-ku ☎492-5151
Mankamerō (Kyō-ryōri) 387, Inokumadōri-Demizu-agaru, Kamigyō-ku ☎441-5020
Mampukuji Temple (Fucha-ryōri) 34, Gokashō-Sambanwari, Uji-shi ☎0774-32-3900
Maruyama (Kaiseki-ryōri) Ike-no-hotori, Maruyama-kōen, Higashiyama-ku ☎561-1991
Matsuba (Udon) Higashi-zume, Shijō-Ōhashi, Higashiyama-ku ☎561-1451
Matsuzushi (Sushi) Takoyakushi, Yanaginobannba, Nishi-iru, Nakagyō-ku ☎221-2946
Minokō (Kaiseki-ryōri) 480, Kiyoichō, Gionshimogawara-dōri, Higashiyama-ku ☎561-0328
Mishima-tei (Sukiyaki) Sanjō-sagaru, Teramachidōri, Nakagyō-ku ☎221-0003
Nakemurarō (Kaiseki-ryōri)
509, Gion-Yasaka-jinja-Minami-mon, Higashiyama-ku ☎561-0016
Nishiki (Kyō-ryōri) Arashiyama-Nakanoshima-Kōennai, Ukyōku ☎871-8888
Okinatei (Sukiyaki) Nishi-iru, Takoyakushidōri-Kawaramachi, Nakagyō-ku ☎221-0250
Okutan (Yudōfu) 86-30, Nanzenji-Fukujichō, Sakyō-ku ☎771-8709
Osaitokoro (Kyō-ryōri) 37, Jōdoji-Ishibashichō, Sakyō-ku ☎771-5157
Sa-Ami (Kaiseki-ryōri) Maruyama-Kōen-nai, Higashiyama-ku ☎561-2200
Seryōjaya (Sansai-ryōri) 22, Ōhara-Shōrin-inchō, Sakyō-ku ☎744-2301
Shimogamo Saryō (Kyō-ryōri) 1, Shimogamo-Izumikawachō, Sakyō-ku ☎701-5185
Shirukō (Kyō-ryōri)
Hitosujime-Higashi-iru, Shijō-Kawaramachi-agaru, Shimogyō-ku ☎221-3250
Sushitora (Sushi) Imadegawa-Sembon, Nishi-iru, Kamigyō-ku ☎462-0615
Tankuma-Kitaten (Kyō-ryōri)
355, Shijō-agaru, Kamiyachō,Nishi-Kiyamachidōri, Nakagyō-ku ☎221-6990
Toriijaya (Kaiseki-ryōri) 49, Kurama-Kibunechō, Sakyō-ku ☎741-2231
Warajiya (Eel) Nakagyō-dōri, Hommachi, Higashi-iru, Higashiyama-ku ☎561-1290
Yachiyo (Tempura) 34, Nanzenji-Fukujichō, Sakyō-ku ☎771-4148
Yōshūji (Kyō-ryōri) 1074-2, Kuramahonchō,Sakyō-ku ☎741-2848

● International

Ashiya (Steak) 4-172-13 Kiyomizu, Higashiyama-ku ☎541-7961
Bodegon (Spanish) 1, Saga Tenryūji-Susukinobabachō, Ukyō-ku ☎872-9652
Capital Tōyōtei Honten (French) Shokubutsuen-Kitamonmae, Kita-ku ☎722-2121
Kaiyōtei (Steak) Pont-chō-Shijō-agaru, Nakagyō-ku ☎221-3607
Kawahisa (Western)
Minami, Hitosujime-Higashi-iru, Kiyamachi-Oike-sagaru, Nakagyō-ku ☎211-0888
Le Relais D'Okazaki (French) 6, Okazaki-Saishōjichō, Sakyō-ku ☎761-1326
Lipton Kiyamachi (Italian) Nishikiyamachi-Shijō-agaru, Shimogyō-ku ☎221-1468
Man-yōken (French) Kitagawa Higashi-iru,Shijō-Fuyachō, Shimogyō-ku ☎221-1022
Oranda (French)
Gion Ueda Bldg., Shijō-agaru-kado, Yamatoōji, Higashiyama-ku ☎561-0335
Restaurant Izutsu (Steak) Sanjō-sagaru, Nawatedōri, Higashiyama-ku ☎541-2121
Restaurant Kitayama (Steak) 14, Iwagakakiuchi-chō, Kamigamo,Kita-ku ☎781-4889
Suehiro (Steak) 43, Higashi-Ten-nōchō, Okazaki, Sakyō-ku ☎751-1529
Sukeroku (Steak) Sembon-Nishi-iru-Kitagawa, Imadegawadōri, Kamigyō-ku ☎461-6789
Toen-tei (Chinese) Sijō-sagaru, Kawaramachi, Shimogyō-ku ☎351-4745
Tōka-saikan (Chinese) Nishizume, Shijō-Ōhashi, Shimogyō-ku ☎221-1147
Tsubosaka (Western) 122, Gion-Tominagachō, Higashiyama-ku ☎561-3923

● Coffee Shop · Sweet Shop

Bun-no-suke Jaya (Amazake)	Kōdaiji-mae, Higashiyama-ku	☎561-1972
Chōrakukan (Coffee)	Gion-Maruyama-kōen-nai, Higashiyama-ku	☎561-0001
Inoda Coffee	Nishi, Sakaimachi-Sanjō-kado, Nakagyō-ku	☎221-0507
Kagizen Yoshifusa (Kuzukiri)	264, Kitagawa, Gionchō, Higashiyama-ku	☎561-1818
Kasagiya (Oshiruko)	Ninenzaka, Kiyomizu-Kōdaiji-Masuyachō, Higashiyama-ku	☎561-9562
Kazariya (Aburimochi)	96, Imamiyachō, Murasakino, Kita-ku	☎491-9402

‹NARA› ☎0742

Hirasō (Sushi)	30-1, Imamikadomachi, Nara-shi	☎22-0866
Miyoshino (Udon)	27, Hashimotochō, Nara-shi	☎22-5239
Nara Hotel Bekkan (Western)		
	Kintetsu-Naraeki-nai, 28, Higashimukinakamachi, Nara-shi	☎26-3101
New Kikusui (Japanese & French)	1130, Takabatakechō Nara-shi	☎23-2007
Shizuka (Kamameshi)	37, Konishichō,Nara-shi	☎22-8029
Tō-no-Chaya (Chagayu)	47, Noboriōjichō, Nara-shi	☎22-4348
Tsukihitei (Kaiseki-ryōri)	158, Kasuganochō, Nara-shi	☎26-2021
Yanagi-Jaya (Kaiseki-ryōri)	Sarusawachihan, 4-49, Noboriōji, Nara-shi	☎23-4763

‹OSAKA› ☎06

Alaska (French) Asahi Shimbun Bldg.,	3-2-4, Nakanoshima, Kita-ku, Osaka-shi	☎231-1351
Hanafusa (French)	4-1-6, Kitakyūhōjichō, Chūō-ku, Osaka-shi	☎252-8723
Honfuku-zushi (Sushi)	1-12, Shinsaibashi-suji, Chūō-ku, Osaka-shi	☎211-5300
Isomura (French)	9-20, Toganochō, Kita-ku, Osaka-shi	☎312-3780
Kagairō (Kaiseki-ryōri)	1-1-14, Kitahama, Chūō-ku, Osaka-shi	☎231-7214
Kicchō (Kaiseki-ryōri)	5-3-68, Nakanoshima, Kita-ku, Osaka-shi	☎448-3168
Kikuya (Tempura) Shin-Hankyū Bldg., 1-12-39, Umeda, Kita-ku, Osaka-shi		☎345-4412
Kuidaore (Restaurant Complex)	1-8-25, Dōtombori,Chūō-ku, Osaka-shi	☎211-5300
Maruman (Sushi)	1-9-3, Dōtombori, Chūō-ku, Osaka-shi	☎211-6197
Maruman Honke (Uosuki)	30, Unagidani-Nakanochō, Chūō-ku, Osaka-shi	☎252-0651
Matsubaya (Udon)	3-8-1, Minami-Semba, Chūō-ku, Osaka-shi	☎251-3339
Meijiken (Western)	1-5-32, Shinsaibashi-suji, Chūō-ku, Osaka-shi	☎271-6761
Mimiu (Udonsuki)	4-6-18, Hiranomachi,Chūō-ku, Osaka-shi	☎231-5770
Nadaman (Japanese) Royal Hotel, 5-3-68, Nakanoshima, Kita-ku, Osaka-shi		☎443-7101
Restaurant Palace La Cour (French)		
	Shinhankyū Bldg, 12F, 1-12-39, Umeda, Kita-ku, Osaka-shi	☎345-4840
Shōben Tangotei (Osaka-ryōri)	1-7-12, Dōtombori, Chūō-ku, Osaka-shi	☎211-3208
Zuboraya (Japanese)	2-5-5, Ebisu-Higashi, Naniwa-ku, Osaka-shi	☎633-5529

‹KOBE› ☎078

Aburiniku-Kōbō-Wakkoku (Steak)	1-22-13, Nakayamatedōri, Chūō-ku, Kobe-shi	☎222-0678
Bistro du Lyon (French)	2-13-6, Yamamotodōri, Chūō-ku, Kobe-shi	☎221-2727
El Pancho Kitano (Spanish)	3-2-4, Kitanochō, Chūō-ku, Kobe-shi	☎241-1344
Itō Grill (Western)	1-6-6, Motomachi, Chūō-ku, Kobe-shi	☎331-2818
Minsei Kanton Ryōriten (Chinese)	1-3-3, Motomachidōri, Chūō-ku, Kobe-shi	☎331-5435
Ōi-nikuten (Steak)	7-2-5, Motomachi, Chūō-ku, Kobe-shi	☎351-1011
Rengatei (Steak)	2-5-5, Shimoyamatedōri, Chūō-ku, Kobe-shi	☎392-2941
Swiss Chalet (Swiss)	3-2-4, Kitanochō, Chūō-ku, Kobe-shi	☎221-4343
Shiburi-jaya (Ochazuke)	3-9-4, Motomachidōri, Chūō-ku, Kobe-shi	☎331-0070

SHOPPING

Whether you are looking for products that reflect centuries of craftsmanship or the latest fruits of high technology, you're sure to find it in Japan.

WHERE TO SHOP

Although not always the cheapest places, department stores offer variety and dependable quality — all in one convenient location. They are also great places just to browse, and most hold regular art and handicraft exhibitions. Souvenir shops can be found in hotel shopping arcades and around tourist attractions and many offer duty-free shopping. Department stores and major shops also offer delivery and shipping services.

HOW TO BUY

● *DUTY-FREE SHOPPING*

Some items may be purchased duty-free (see the list below) at authorized shops upon presentation of your passport. When you make a duty-free purchase you are given a form called the 'Record of Commodities Tax Exempt for Export'. This should be kept to show customs officials when leaving the country. If you ship a duty-free item, you must show proof to customs. The exemption rate in 5% to 40%.

1. Precious stones.
2. Pearls, articles decorated with pearls.
3. Articles made or plated with precious metals.
4. Cloisonne and articles made of tortoise shell, coral and amber ivory.
5. Furs and household implements made of fiber.
6. Hunting guns and fishing tackle.
7. TV sets, projectors and screens, video recorders and players.
8. Radios, tape recorders, hi-fi eqipment.
9. Cameras, motion picture cameras and projectors, including photometers, lenses, bodies and tripods.
10. Timepieces, including those with cases decorated with gold, platinum and other precious metals.
11. Smoking utensils.
12. Passenger vehicles.
13. Dolls, doll cases and toys.

● *CREDIT CARDS*

Credit cards are honored at

department stores and major shops. American Express, Visa International and Master Card are the most frequently accepted. Department stores and major souvenir shops are also authorized money changers.

WHAT TO BUY

Whatever you choose to buy, a generally high standard of workmanship and quality is assured. Some suggestions are:

● CHINAWARE

Ranging from purely utilitarian to extravagantly ornamental, Japanese china is some of the best in the world and that produced in Kyoto is no exception. Kyoto's chinaware, *Kyō-yaki* has two main types, *Awata-yaki* and the dominant style, *Kiyomizu-yaki*. *Awata-yaki* gained popularity due to the creativity and workmanship of **Kuemon Sanmojiya** while *Kiyomizu-yaki* owes its fame to *Nonomura Ninsei*. Both were master potters of the Edo era and *Ninsei* is said to have had a sense of color and form amounting to genius. Since the Edo era numerous developments and improvements have been introduced.

● *SHIKKI (LAQUERWARE)*

Kyoto Laquerware, with its elegant designs and sturdy construction is regarded as the highest form of this art and Kyoto is especially well-known for the gold and silver laquer work called *makié*. Created in the Momoyama era, this elaborate style was favored by the Imperial court and the nobility, which encouraged the progress of the art. The success and style of *makié* is attributed to the 17th C masters *Hon-ami Kōetsu* and *Kōrin Ogata*.

● *SILK FABRICS*

Kyoto has long been associated with the art of silk weaving, particularly the luxurious fabrics produced by the *Nishijin* weaving method. *Nishijin* is the area of Kyoto where weavers congregated in the late 15th C and fabrics are still manufactured in this area today, mostly in the craftmen's own homes.

The silk weaving industry first appeared in Kyoto in the 8th C and developed under the encouragement of the Imperial court. Methods introduced by Chinese artisans were quickly adapted by Kyoto weavers, who began to produce gauze, brocade, damask, satin and crepe. The Nishijin quarter supplied the Imperial court and was later fostered by the Tokugawa

173

government.

The dyed silk fabrics known as *Yūzen-zome* are a specialty of Kyoto and the dyeing method was perfected by the 17th C painter *Miyazaki Yūzen*. His method influenced the entire nation with its brilliant colors and novel designs.

● *FOLDING FANS*

The *Ōgi*, or folding fan, is made of paper glued onto thin bamboo ribs pinned at the base to form a pivot and are decorated with various designs. They were originally produced in the Heian era and now Kyoto produces about 60% of the country's folding fans. These beautifully decorated fans make ideal room ornaments.

● *DOLLS*

Traditional Kyoto dolls have been produced since the Heian era and are representative products of the city. One well-known type features graceful, beautifully clad dolls representing figures of the Imperial court and nobility. Also famous are *Ichimatsu* dolls, first produced in the Edo era as representations of the *kabuki* actor *Sanogawa Ichimatsu*. With their black, classically cut hair and chubby cheeks, these dolls have enjoyed great popularity.

Other traditional Kyoto products include woodblock prints, cloisonne and damascene work, Buddhist altar fittings and bamboo crafts.

● *PEARLS*

Cultured pearls were developed in Japan by *Kōkichi Mikimoto*. Each piece of jewelry is designed with the utmost care.

● *PAPER LANTERNS*

Once actually used to light rooms, these are now mostly used for inferior decoration.

● *CAMERAS AND OPTICALS*

Japanese cameras are world famous. Buy them and other audio visual goods in duty-free shops.

Name	address	Tel.	P.

〈**KYOTO**〉 ☎075

● *Department Stores*

Daimaru	79, Tachiuri-Nishimachi, Shijō-Takakura-Nishi-iru, Shimogyō-ku	☎211-8111
Fujii-Daimaru	605, Teianmaenochō, Teramachidōri-Shijō-sagaru, Shimogyō-ku	☎221-8181
Hankyū	68, Shinchō, Shijōdōri-Kawaramachi-Higashi-iru, Shimogyō-ku	☎223-2288
Kintetsu	702, Shiokōjichō, Karasumadōri-Shichijō-sagaru-Higashi Shimogyō-ku	☎361-1111
Takashimaya	52, Shinchō, Shijō-Kawaramachi-Nishi-iru Shimogyō-ku	☎221-8811

● *Japanese Goods*

Choboya (Zōri)	Hanamikōji-Shijō-agaru, Higashiyama-ku	☎561-5584

Erizen (Kimono)	49, Shijō-Otabichō, Shimogyō-ku	☎221-1618
Higashiyama Kōgei (Folkcraft)	Kōdaiji-Kitamon-Higashi-iru, Higashiyama-ku	☎561-5473
Itō Kumihimo (Cord)	Teramachi-Rokkaku-Hokusei-kado, Nakagyō-ku	☎221-1320
Kawabun (Japanese Paper)		
	576, Gionmachi-Minamigawa, Higashiyama-ku	☎561-0277
Kodai Yūzen-en (Yūzen-dyeing)	Takatsujidōri-Inokuma-Nishi-iru, Shimogyōku	☎823-0500
Kyoto Handicraft Center	Higashi, Kumano-Jinja, Sakyō-ku	☎761-5080
Miyawaki Baisen-an (Fan)		
	Rokkaku-Tominokōji-Nishi-iru, 73, Daikokuchō, Nakagyō-ku	☎221-0181
Morita Washi (Japanese paper)		
	Higashitōin-Bukkōji-agaru, Shimogyō-ku	☎341-0123
Nakamura Chingireten (Folkcraft)		
	Nawatedori-Sanjō-Minami-iru, Higashiyama-ku	☎561-4726
Nihon Shishū Yakata (Embroidery)		
	36, Nishi-kyōgoku-Nishikoromodechō, Ukyō-ku	☎313-2151
Nijūsnaya (Comb)	Shijōkawaramachi-Higashi-iru,Shinmachi, Shimogyō-ku	☎221-2371
Nishijin Textile Center (Nishijin Textile)		
	Horikawadōri-Imadegawa-Minami-iru, Kamigyō-ku	☎451-9231
Okamoto Orimonoten (Kimono)	I-chōme, Kiyomizu-Shim-michi, Higashiyama-ku	☎561-4436

● Foods

Doi Shibazuke-Hompo (Pickles)	41, Yasehanajirichō, Sakyō-ku	☎744-2311
Fūke(Yuba)	Nishinotōin-Shimotachiuri-sagaru, Kamigyō-ku	☎231-1584
Kambayashi Shunshō Honten (Uji-cha)	38, Ujimyōraku, Uji-shi	☎0774-22-2514
Kameyamutsu (Confectionery)		
	153, Hishiya-machi, Nishinakasuji-dōri, Shichijō, Shimogyō-ku	☎371-1447
Kawabata Dōki (Confectionary)		
	2-12, Minami Nonogamichō,Shimogamo, Sakyō-ku	☎781-8117
Mametomi Hompo (Confectionery)		
	Nishi, Higashinakasuji-Shichijō-agaru, Shimogyō-ku	☎371-2850
Matsumaeya (Sea Tangle)	Kamaza -Marutamachi, Nakagyō-ku	☎231-4233
Morika (Tōfu)	42, Sagashakadō-Fujinokichō, Ukyō-ku	☎872-3955
Murakami Kaishindō (Cake)	Higashigawa, Teramachi-Nijō-agaru, Nakagyō-ku	☎231-1058
Shichimiya (Tōgarashi)	2-221, Kiyomizu, Higashiyama-ku	☎551-0738
Sugukiya Rokurobee (Pickles)	Kamigamo-Jinja-Toriimae, Kita-ku	☎721-6669
Tawaraya Yoshitomi (Confectionery)		
	Muromachidōri-Kamidachiuri-agaru, Kamigyō-ku	☎432-2211
Toraya Kurokawa (Confectionery)	Karasumadōri-Ichijō-kado, Kamigyō-ku	☎441-3111
Tsuruya Yoshinobu (Confectionery)		
	Kita, Imadegawadōri-Horikawa-Nishi-iru, Kamigyō-ku	☎441-0105

● Potery · Ceramics

Asahidō (Ceramics)	1-280, Kiyomizu, Higashiyama-ku	☎531-2181
Ebiya Ryūzan(Ceramics)	Gojōzaka Kiyomizu, Pool Bus-tei-mae, Higashiyama-ku	☎551-3883
Inaba (Cloisonné)	Sanjo-Shirakawabashi, Nishi-iru, Higashiyama-ku	☎761-1161
Kotobuki Tōshun (Ceramics)	7-2, Kiyomizuyaki-Danchichō, Yamashina-ku	☎581-7195
Kyoto Tōjiki Kaikan (Ceramics)	Gojōzaka, Higashiyama-ku	☎541-1102
Tachikichi (Ceramics)	Shijō-Tominokōji-kado, Shimogyō-ku	☎211-3141
Zōhiko (Lacquer Ware)	10, Okazaki-Saishōjimachi, Sakyō-ku	☎752-7777

● Doll · Silk Fabrics

Kanebō Boutique (Silk)	Kawaramachi-Shijō-agaru, Nakagyō-ku	☎221-7927

Nishimura (Silk)
381, Motochō, Furumonzendōri-Yamatoōji Higashi-iru, Higashiyama-ku ☎561-1312
Matsuya (Doll) Higashigawa, Kawaramachi-Shijō-agaru, Nakagyō-ku ☎221-5902
Iura Ningyōten (Doll) 2,Saga-ogurayamachō, Ukyō-ku ☎871-7141
Tanakaya (Doll) Shijōdōri-Yanaginobaba-Higashi-iru, Shimogyō-ku ☎221-1959
Tanka (Doll) 22-504, Honmachi, Higashiyama-ku ☎561-1627
Tatsumura (Silk) 29, Mibumorimachi, Nakagyō-ku ☎802-3251

● Pearls
Komai (Pearl)
261, Shinmozen-Higashiōji-nishiiru, Umemotochō, Higashiyama-ku ☎541-8171

● Unique Goods
Fūgadō (Lantern) 3-331-1, Kiyomizu, Higashiyama-ku ☎551-0713
Garacia (Glass) 10, Koyama Nishimotomachi, Kita-iru ☎491-4689
Ishikawa Take-no-mise (Bamboo Goods)
35, Tsukurimichichō, Saga-tenryūji, Ukyō-ku ☎861-0076
Naitō Rikimatsu Shōten (Hemp-palm Broom)
Kita, Sanjō-Ōhashi-Nishizume, Nakagyō-ku ☎221-3018
Mikumo (Woodblock Prints) Kita, Shijō-Nakashindō-nishiiru, Nakagyō-ku ☎841-3478
Shōeidō (Incense) Higashigawa, Karasumadōri-Nijō-agaru, Nakagyō-ku ☎231-2307
Tsujikura (Paper Umbrella) Kawaramachi-Shijō-agaru, Nakagyō-ku ☎221-4396

● Cameras
Matsumidō Shijō-Kawaramachi-Higashi-iru, Shimogyō-ku ☎231-4384
Sakuraya Sanjō-Kawaramachi-Rokkaku, Nakagyō-ku ☎221-0721

〈NARA〉 ☎0742
Chiyonoya Takemura (Confectionery) 22, Minamimachi, Higashimuki, Nara-shi ☎22-2325
Genrindō (Ink Stick) 2-3-12, Saikujōchō, Nara-shi ☎63-0255
Ikeda Gankōdō (Fan) 16, Sanjōdōri, Tsunofurichō, Nara-shi ☎22-3690
Kobaien (Ink Stick) 7, Tsubaichō, Nara-shi ☎23-2965
Mori Narazuketen (Pickles) 23, Kasuganochō, Nara-shi ☎26-2063

〈OSAKA〉 ☎06
Daimaru (Department Store) 3-1-1, Umeda,Kita-ku, Osaka-shi ☎343-1231
Hankyū (Department Store) 8-7, Kakutachō, Kita-ku, Osaka-shi ☎361-1381
Hanshin (Department Store) 1-13-13, Umeda, Kita-ku, Osaka-shi ☎345-1201
Sogō (Department Store) 1-8-3, Shinsaibashisuji, Chūō-ku, Osaka-shi ☎281-3111
Sōhonke Tsuriganeya (Confectionery) 1-5-2, Daidō, Tennōji-ku Osaka-shi ☎771-0044
Tsunosei (Confectionary) 1-Higashi-6-21, Dōtombori, Chūō-ku, Osaka-shi ☎211-1151

〈KOBE〉 ☎078
Daimaru (Department Store) 40, Akashi-chō, Chūō-ku, Kobe-shi ☎331-8121
Hankyū (Department Store) 4-2-1, Kanō-chō, Chūō-ku, Kobe-shi ☎321-3521
Marukiya (Antique) 3-3-21, Yamamotodōri, Chūō-ku, Kobe-shi ☎231-8726
Mikimoto Pearl Island (Pearl) 1-7-1, Toba, Toba-shi ☎0599-25-2028
One Way (Stationery) 3-11-15, Kitanagasadōri, Chūō-ku, Kobe-shi ☎331-3378
Primtemps (Department Store) 8-1-2, Kumoi-dōri, Chūō-ku, Kobe-shi ☎291-0077
Sogō (Department Store) 8-1-8, Onoe-dōri, Chūō-ku, Kobe-shi ☎221-4181

ENTERTAINMENT

Everyone has a favorite way of spending their free time and Kyoto offers entertainment to suit all tastes. Tickets to theater and other events can be obtained at "Playguides" in department stores, or at the venue itself.

CLASSICAL DRAMA

● KABUKI

Melodramatic plays enlivened by songs and dances, *Kabuki* employs bold, exaggerated make-up and costumes with brilliant colors. Although all the actors are now male, *Kabuki* was actually created in the 17th C by a woman named *Okuni* who was attached to Izumo Shrine. Woman were banned from performing by the shogunate, forcing the adoption of all male casts and creating the infamous *onnagata* or *oyama* (men playing woman's roles). Throughout the Edo era, *Kabuki* was entertainment for the common man and these days it still thrives as drama which displays the vitality of the Japanese spirit.

● NOH

A narrative in dance, *Noh* relies heavily on the abstract. The stage is almost bare of props and the main characters are masked. The word *Noh* simply means performance and *Noh* developed from an older dramatic form called *sarugaku*. It has kept its present form since the 15th century. In contrast to *Kabuki, Noh* was the entertainment of the aristocracy, so the dances are often stately and elegant. Like *Kabuki* (which was greatly influenced by *Noh*), performances are long but the serious dramas are interspersed with comical plays called *kyōgen*. Verging on slapstick, they are designed as relief from the serious themes dealt with in *Noh*.

● BUNRAKU

Bunraku is a unique style of puppet theater, employing elaborate and exquisitely dressed dolls. The dolls are about 50 cm tall and have built-in mechanisms to aid movement. They are skillfully manipulated to act out an entertaining narrative to the accompaniment of *shamisen* music. Usually, three puppeteers operate one puppet and the master puppeteer

177

is often dressed in a brilliant *kimono* while the assistants wear black in order to act as a foil to their leader and the colorful puppets. *Bunraku* can be seen at the National Bunraku Theater in Osaka.

● KYO - MAI (KYOTO DANCING)

From the 8th C onwards, Kyoto was the center of Japanese culture and so various performing arts were born here, most cultivated and promoted by the aristocracy. These arts were either elegant and refined or dazzling in their showmanship and the most famous of them are the exquisite dances performed by the *maiko* and *geiko* of Gion. Performances include the *Miyako-odori*, held from April 1—30; the *Kitano-odori*, held from April 15—25; and the *Kamogawa-odori*, held from May 1—24 and from October 15 — November 7. Ticket reservations for performances can be made at travel agencies.

MOVIES

Movie theaters abound in entertainment districts of Osaka and Kyoto, and include large, first-run theaters showing both domestic and foreign films. Admission fees range from ¥1,600 up to ¥2,500 for a reserved seat.

THEATER

● VARIETY THEATER

In Japan's traditional variety theater, a range of popular entertainments is offered including *rakugo* (comic storytelling), *kōdan* (dramatic narration) and *kijutsu* (conjuring). A very popular entertainment in Osaka is *Kamigata manzai*, a comic dialog, in the Osaka dialect, between two comedians. This can be seen at the Umeda Kagetsu and Namba Kagetsu theaters.

CONCERTS

There is always a wide variety of concert performances to choose from in Japan with everything from symphony orchestras to rock groups, both domestic and foreign. The Japanese are a nation of music lovers and every kind of music has a following here. Kyoto boasts many long-established live houses in the city area.

SPORTS

● BASEBALL

Baseball has a tremendous following in Japan and like the U.S.A., it has 2 major leagues: the Pacific League and the Central League. In the Kinki Region, the major professional teams are the Kintetsu

Buffaloes, the Orix Blue Wave and the Hanshin Tigers. The playing season is from April to October.

● *SUMO*

Ranking in popularity with baseball, *Sumō* is Japan's national sport and is always an exciting spectacle. The professional wrestlers are powerfully built, usually weighing between 130 and 150 kg. *Sumō* tournaments are held in Osaka in March at the Osaka Furitsu Taiikukan Hall.

● *JUDO*

Jūdō is Japan's best-known sport and another system of fighting without weapons. *Jūdō* has developed into an Olympic sport.

Name	address	Tel.
⟨KYOTO⟩ ☎075		
Gion Corner (Japanese Show)	570-2, Gionchō-Minamigawa, Highshiyama-ku	☎561-1115
Gion (Kōbu) Kaburenjō(Kyō Dance)		
	570-2, Gionchō-Minamigawa, Higashiyama-ku	☎561-1117
Kanze Kaikan (Noh)	44, Okazaki, Enshōjichō Sakyō-ku	☎771-6114
Kyoto Municipal Museum of Traditional Industry		
	9-2, Okazaki, Seishōjichō Sakyō-ku	☎761-3421
Minamiza Theater (Kabuki)	Higashizume Shijō-Ohashi, Higashiyama-ku	☎561-1155
Miyagawachō Kaburenjō Theater (Kyō Dance)		
	4-306 Miyagawa-suji, Higashiyama-ku	☎561-1151
Nishijin Textile Center (Textile Exhibition)		
	Imadegawa-Minami, Horikawa-dōri, Kamigyō-ku	☎451-9231
Pontochō Kaburenjō Theater (Kyō Dance)	Sanjō-sagaru, Pontochō, Nakagyō-ku	☎221-2025
Seibukan (Budō)	60, Izumikawa-chō, Shimogamo, Sakyō-ku	☎701-3121
Sumiya (Japanese Show)	32, Ageyachō, Nishishinyashiki, Shimogyō-ku	☎351-0024
Sports Vally Kyoto (Amusement Park)	120, Nose-chō, Yase, Sakyō-ku	☎781-9151
Yūzen Cultural Hall (Textile Exhibition)	6, Mametachō, Nishi-Kyōgoku, Ukyō-ku	☎311-0025
N (Nara)☎0742 O (Osaka)☎06 K (Kobe)☎078		
Namba Kagetsu (Engei)	11-6 Sen-nichi-mae, Namba, Chūō-ku, Osaka-shi	O. 641-0888
Nara Dreamland (Amusement Park)	1900, Hōdenchō, Nara-shi	N. 23-1111
National Bunraku Theater (Bunraku)		
	1-12-10, Nihombashi, Chūō-ku, Osaka-shi	O. 212-2531
Osaka Nohgaku Kaikan (Noh)	2-3-17 Nakazaki-Nishi, Kita-ku, Osaka-shi	O. 373-1726
Portpia Land (Amusement Park)		
	8-7-1, Nakamachi, Minatojima, Chūō-ku, Kobe-shi	K. 302-2820
Shin-Kabukiza Theater (Kabuki)	4-3-25, Namba, Chūō-ku, Osaka-shi	O. 631-2121
Takarazuka Grand Theater (Revue)	1-1-57, Sakaemachi, Takarazuka-shi	☎0797-86-7777

179

NIGHTLIFE

Like all Japan's major cities, Kyoto and Osaka have many entertainment areas with an enormous variety of cabarets, night-clubs and bars. High-class nightclubs in Kyoto's Gion area are extraordinarily expensive and visiting them remains the privelege of the very rich.

CLUBS AND CABARETS

Clubs are usually the more expensive and have hostesses serving drinks and providing entertaining conversation. Cabarets are about ¥10,000 to ¥20,000 per person and feature live floor shows. More risque cabarets often employ energetic touts to lure you in. If you intend to be adventurous, be sure to check prices beforehand.

BARS

Inexpensive bars can be found in almost any section of the city. Traditional bars are usually small, friendly and lively and are good places to soak up the local atmosphere along with some *sake or shōchū*.

PUBS

Generally low-priced, pubs differ from bars only in the type of patron they attract and seem to be favored by the younger generation.

DISCOS

Discos flourish in entertainment areas. The cover charge averages between ¥3,000 and ¥5,000 per person.

CAFE-BARS

Cafe-Bars have become increasingly popular and a great variety of interesting places now exist. They serve cocktails, coffee and light meals.

CHAYA

Chaya were originally restaurants serving refreshments to patrons of kabuki but later developed into high-class nightclubs. *Ochaya-asobi* is a dinner party held in a *chaya*, with *maiko* and *geiko* providing entertainment for the guests. There are around 120 *chaya* in Gion but priority is given to regular customers and it is impossible to visit these places without an introduction. The cost is usually around ¥100,000 per guest.

Name	address	Tel.
〈KYOTO〉 ☎075		
Bluenote (Jazz)	BAL Bldg. Kawaramachi-Takoyakushi-agaru, Nakagyō-ku	☎223-0398
Sekisui Bar (Bar)	Nishizume, Kamogawa-Nijō-Ōhashi, Nakagyō-ku	☎222-1511
Juttoku (Live House)	Marutamachi-agaru, Ōmiya, Kamigyō-ku	☎841-1691
Lady Day (Jazz)	Nishikiyamachi-Takoyakushi-agaru, Nakagyō-ku	☎223-2655
Maharaja (Disco)	Gion-Kaikan, 323 Kitagawa Gionchō, Higashiyama-ku	☎541-5421
Moustache (Cafe Bar)	Shizuya Bldg., B1F, Kitagawa Yosujime-Higashi-iru Sanjo-Sagaru, Kawaramachi Nakagyō-ku	☎222-0031
Starlight Bar (Bar)	Nijōjō-mae, Horikawa-dōri, Nakagyō-ku	☎222-1111
Yamafuku (Sake)	Hitosujime-Higashi-iru Gionhanamikōji-Shijō-sagaru, Higashiyama-ku	☎551-0876
〈OSAKA〉 ☎06		
Kimura Bar	1-6-21, Sonezaki-Shinchi, Kita-ku, Osaka-shi	☎345-3659
Patina (Disco)	B2F Hotel Nikkō Osaka,1-3-3, Nishi-Shinsaibashi, Chūō-ku, Osaka-shi	☎244-1111
West Coast (Wine)	Hankyū-Grand Bldg., 8-47 Kadota-chō, Kita-ku, Osaka-shi	☎315-7780
Yoshida Bar (Bar)	2-4-6, Nanba, Chuō-ku, Osaka-shi	☎213-1385
〈KOBE〉 ☎078		
Et toi (Live House)	3-8-12, Sannomiyachō, Chūō-ku, Kobe-shi	☎332-1755
Kings Arms (Pub)	4-2-15, Isobedōri, Chūō-ku, Kobe-shi	☎221-3774
New München (Pub)	2-5-18, Sannomiyachō, Chūō-ku, Kōbe-shi	☎391-0360
Pleind Etoiles (Sky Lounge)	6-10-1, Minatojima-Nakamachi, Chūō-ku, Kobe-shi	☎302-1111
The Attic (Pub)	Ijinkan Club, 4-1-12, Kitanochō, Chūō-ku, Kōbe-shi	☎222-5368
Gen (Chinese Pub)	1-7-1, Shinoharahonmachi, Nada-ku, Kōbe-shi	☎882-4520

181

SIGHTSEEING

TRAVEL GUIDE KYOTO

Nara·Osaka·Kobe
〈英文京都案内〉

1993年8月1日　改訂15版発行
編集人　神部　隆志
発行人　岩田　光正
発行所　JTB 日本交通公社出版事業局

〒150 東京都渋谷区道玄坂1-10-8
渋谷野村ビル7階☎03-3477-9566

●スタッフ
企画編集　JTB編集二部 外語図書編集部
　　　　　担当編集長　黒澤明夫
取材・編集協力　㈱アーバン・トランスレーション
地図制作　㈱千秋社
写真協力　JTBフォト
表紙カバー・イラスト　東芳純
翻訳　LINC Japan Ltd. Brian O'Flaherty

JTB発行の図書のご注文は
JTB出版販売センター
〒150 東京都渋谷区道玄坂1-10-8
渋谷野村ビル7階☎03-3477-9588
写真植字　株式会社デンプロ
印刷所　凸版印刷株式会社

JTB For Your TraveLife

184

ISBN4-533-01357-0